Language and Learning:
An Interactional Perspective

EDUCATIONAL ANALYSIS
General Editors: Philip Taylor and Colin Richards

CONTEMPORARY ANALYSIS IN EDUCATION SERIES
General Editor: Philip Taylor

Contemporary Analysis in Education Series

Language and Learning: An Interactional Perspective

Edited and Introduced by
Gordon Wells
University of Bristol

John Nicholls
University of East Anglia

 The Falmer Press

(A member of the Taylor & Francis Group)
London and Philadelphia

UK	The Falmer Press, Falmer House, Barcombe, Lewes, East Sussex, BN8 5DL
USA	The Falmer Press, Taylor & Francis Inc., 242 Cherry Street, Philadelphia, PA 19106-1906

First published 1985

Library of Congress Cataloging in Publication Data

Main entry under title:

Language and Learning.

   (Contemporary Analysis in Education Series)
   Bibliography: p.
   1. Language and Education—Addresses, essays, lectures.
2. Language Acquisition—Addresses, essays, lectures.
3. Learning—Addresses, essays, lectures. 4. Socio-
linguistics—Addresses, essays, lectures. I. Wells, C. Gordon.
II. Nicholls, John. III. Series.
P40.8.L366 1985 401'.9 85-6728
ISBN 1-85000-028-X

Typeset in 11/13 Garamond by
Imago Publishing Ltd, Thame, Oxon.

Jacket design by Leonard Williams

Printed in Great Britain by Taylor & Francis (Printers) Ltd, Basingstoke

Contents

Contents

General Editor's Preface

Coleridge is reputed to have said: 'But still the heart doth need a language' and one might add 'So does the mind and the hands', though not if one realises how completely language and learning possess a deep mutual dependency. Heart, mind and hands interact with language to make learning possible. It is on this interactional perspective that this book is based. Each of its contributors sharpens our appreciation of how very fully learning depends on language of all kinds — spoken, written, heard *and* seen. The contributors also show how very important it is if this dependency is to be a means to opening and not closing windows on the many worlds of human-being that those most dependent — the young, the culturally deprived and the poorly educated — should find ready collaborators in their search not only for autonomy of mind, but also freedom of spirit.

From a basis in the history of the search for the key to the relationship between language and learning and the growing realization that the one is crucial to the other, this collection of original papers takes one into the excitement that is the study of language in learning. Each in its own way, every contribution is authoritative and leaves the reader with a sense of wonder that so much is becoming known, yet there remains so much to know. It is this sense of being at the cutting edge of knowledge that distinguishes this collection of papers. They represent both for the scholar and the student and updating and a perspective of value on a subject — language and learning — that is at the heart of the educational process.

Gordon Wells and John Nicholls are certainly to be congratu-lated for the coherence they have given this volume, but more for the valuable accessibility they have provided for the student of language and education.

Philip Taylor
Birmingham 1984

Editors' Introduction

John Nicholls and Gordon Wells

The original brief for this collection of papers asked us to seek contributions exploring: 'Implications for education of advances over the past twenty-five years in our understanding of language'. During those years, in our opinion, educational understanding of the role of language in learning has been transformed and the papers we have collected are intended to show what we mean by that claim.

In the late 1950s and early 1960s in both Britain and the United States, education was coming under increasing scrutiny — though for rather different reasons. Post-war social idealism in Britain had produced a successful scheme to provide medical care for everyone. The intention to provide secondary education for all children had not proved so successful, however, for it was becoming only too clear that among working class families academic success was effectively being limited to a disproportionately small number of children. Concern about this began to direct attention to the educational process — to questions about the way children learn and how teaching takes account of this. In the United States, on the other hand, there was growing concern that schools were not producing enough people equipped to contribute to the development of new technology — a concern exacerbated by the Russian success with Sputnik. The immediate effect of this emphasis on educational product was to direct attention to the curriculum, especially of secondary schools, rather than on to the learning process.

Both causes of concern were soon influencing educational thinking on both sides of the Atlantic and, in Britain, the Crowther Report (Central Advisory Council for Education, 1959) illustrates this. It was published exactly twenty-five years ago and according to the Introduction, was about 'The education of English boys and girls aged from fifteen to eighteen years'. In those days compulsory schooling ended at fifteen, hence — or so the writers claimed — 'most of them are not being educated'. All, however, were required to register for National Service at eighteen, so it was not difficult to survey educational attainment among a representative sample of eighteen year olds.

The report made it very clear that success or failure in school had less to do with measured intelligence than with other factors that were associated with social class membership and family background. Although it did not go on to claim that language accounted for the failure of so many children from 'working class' families, language was already recognized as a potential source of learning difficulty in the study of science. A secondary education it was argued, should ensure that pupils who specialized in arts subjects gained a better understanding of science — they needed to acquire a basic 'numeracy'. This new term was defined as 'a general understanding of scientific method and language'.

Four years later, the Newsom Report (Central Advisory Council for Education, 1963) considered 'education between the ages of twelve and sixteen of pupils of average and less than average ability'. The majority were still leaving school at fifteen and most of these were the children of working class families. The cause of this social class difference was now clearly attributed to language difference and the children of working class families were envisaged as being 'linguistically disadvantaged'. In the words of the Report:

> There is much unrealized talent among these boys and girls whose potential is masked by inadequate powers of speech and the limitations of home background.

That beguiling explanation for failure in school has continued to influence educational thinking and practice ever since. Fortunately it has also stimulated an enormous amount of research and, because of this, the connection between language, social class and educational success is no longer seen in such simple, not to say insulting, terms.

Developments in the Study of Child Language

Until the early 1960s people who wished to take account of the role of language in child development and learning could not easily find much to help them in the currently published work of linguists. But from then onwards the position changed very rapidly. It is now possible to distinguish four kinds of theoretical emphasis which have contributed to this growth of understanding:

1 a focus on the grammar of language;
2 relating language learning to cognitive development more generally;
3 exploring the social and pragmatic contexts of language learning and use;
4 foregrounding the interpersonal and interactive nature of language learning.

Proponents of these different views often saw their own as opposed to any other, but collectively they have transformed educational understanding of the role of language in learning. The brief account which follows attempts to show what was new about each of them. (For a fuller account see Chapter 2 of Wells, 1981.)

1. *Transformational-generative grammar and the development of syntax*

The renewed interest in language development began almost exactly twenty-five years ago as a direct result of the publication of Chomsky's (1959) critique and refutation of Skinner's then influential behaviourist account of language learning. In this and in his subsequent works (for example, 1965; 1976), Chomsky gave a new direction to linguistic research with syntax as a central concern. Command of a language was seen as requiring knowledge of rules for combining and ordering syntactically defined categories; these were held to be essential in order to account for the relationship that holds between meaning and sound. Three sets of rules are involved in transformational-generative grammar: *phrase structure* rules, which generate the underlying or 'deep structure', to which meaning is related (seen as universal in all languages); *transformation* rules, which operate on the output of the phrase structure rules to derive the 'surface structure'; this is then realized through the application of *phonological* rules as the sequences of sounds that make up the sentences of a particular language.

This precise description of syntactic rules also happened to coincide with the development of portable tape recorders and, as a result, many studies of natural conversation were undertaken in order to investigate the sequence in which various grammatical structures were learned. The most comprehensive of these studies was undertaken in the United States by Brown and his colleagues during the 1960s although the results did not become widely known until the publication of *A First Language* (Brown, 1973).

Transformational-generative grammar was more than a description; it was also a theory about a native speaker's knowledge of language — called a speaker's 'competence'. The theory was of special interest to education, because it seemed to have implications about how competence is acquired. Chomsky was much concerned to emphasize the extremely abstract nature of the rules which constitute a speaker's competence. Such is their complexity, he argued, and so speedily are they acquired by very young children, that an explanation of their acquisition could not be provided by an behaviourist theory of learning. Chomsky's alternative explanation was that every human child is born with a 'Language Acquisition Device'.

2. Cognition and the semantics of language development

Unlike the case with the previous emphasis, there was no single founding father for this new direction in the study of language development. This is hardly surprising, because it drew on work in both linguistics and psychology and, by doing so, drew attention to a very different type of transformation — the transformation of pre-linguistic sensori-motor intelligence into the kind of symbolic thinking that language demands. It took from linguistics the semantic categories proposed by Fillmore (1968) for a 'case grammar' and from psychology many features of the all-pervading developmental theory of Piaget (for example Piaget and Inhelder, 1969). Work based on this 'cognition hypothesis' (Slobin, 1973; Cromer, 1979) soon raised questions about the need to postulate a language-specific acquisition device — even though the behaviourist account of initial language learning continued to be rejected. At the same time, the cognition hypothesis also drew attention to the two-way relationship between language and thinking. Cognitive psychology can certainly account for the way sensori-motor intelligence enables a young child to break into the language code but language, once acquired, is itself a major means of extending the range and complexity of thought (Brown, 1973).

Recognition of the fact that, in early utterances, a child may mean more than he is able to express led to a greater attention being paid to the context of utterance and to the use of the method of 'rich interpretation' to infer the child's semantic intention. Bloom (1970) was the first to adopt this approach whole-heartedly and the now famous example of her daughter's two utterances of 'mummy-sock' provides clear evidence of language being used to express relational meanings which could only have been derived from studying the context. The words were identical in each case but the meaning was entirely different — something like 'That's mummy's sock' on one occasion and 'Mummy's putting on my sock' on the other.

3. Social semiotics and the pragmatics of language development

The cognition hypothesis tended to focus attention on the difference between sensori-motor intelligence and subsequent thinking, with particular reference to Piaget's developmental theory. The model of thinking which this entailed, however, was mainly concerned with logico-mathematical reasoning which, although important in later development, gives a very unbalanced picture of the early stages of language learning. In a child's early experience it is the interpersonal and social aspect of communication that predominates — the pragmatic functions served by the utterances that are produced and responded to.

To explore the interpersonal and pragmatic functions of language directs attention away from the contexts of early words to the contexts of even earlier experiences and the purposes that 'pre-lingustic' utterances serve. Here the work of Halliday (1975a) has been a major influence. He too studied his own child, Nigel, but — unlike Bloom — he treated the emergence of stable 'vocalization-meaning' pairs as the beginning of language. In Nigel's case, these emerged at the age of nine months and the 'meanings' his parents attributed to these utterances were entirely pragmatic. They were interpreted as designed to serve the interpersonal purposes that Nigel wished to achieve. Halliday's functional categories emphasize language as 'meaning potential' — as a cultural resource for social interaction, which has its origins in the often idiosyncratic and ritualized interchanges between a child and his/her parents or primary care-givers.

The work of Bruner (1975) has been another very important influence on the development of understanding of this aspect of early communication. His emphasis on the pre-linguistic antecedents of early language also drew attention to something that continues throughout the second year of life and indeed well beyond it, namely that most children seem able to comprehend far more complex utterances than they can produce. It has been suggested that this asymmetry begins with differences in the communicative aims of parents and children (Wells, 1981). What is certain, however, is the young child's desire to succeed in communicating — something that can even be seen in the gestures of babies as well as in the pre-linguistic vocalizations of infants and in their subsequently structured utterances containing recognizable words. Such a view runs counter to Piaget's claim that very young children are essentially egocentric — perhaps they only appear to be so if the observing adult does not engage in an interpersonal relationship with them?

4. Inter-subjectivity and the personal basis of initial language learning

It is commonly claimed (and often treated as ridiculous) that mothers understand what their babies mean almost from the day they are born. Recent research suggests this is hardly surprising, since mothers attribute meaning to what to others seem no more than their babies' random gurgles and movements. That is to say they treat what are initially involuntary acts as if they were intentional and, by doing so, establish that inter-subjectivity which is probably the basis of all subsequent communicative development. The truly extraordinary achievement of almost all mothers and babies is that, within a very few weeks, they establish patterns of interaction involving gaze, gesture and often vocal sounds as well, in what Trevarthen (1978) has called 'proto-conversations'.

Trevarthen's study involved video-recordings made in the laboratory of mother's interactions with their babies. Normally, of course, such interactions arise during the routines of feeding, bathing and dressing, when a baby is awake and comfortable and has other people around. That is to say, learning takes place in a social context in which adults respond to the baby's behaviour by vocalizing, smiling, touching and looking wherever the baby looks. The adult responsiveness provides the motivation and the necessary support for this social learning.

As Shields (1978) argues, to take part in, and to learn from, social interaction requires the development of sophisticated communication skills. These, in their turn, entail the development of cognitive schemes about oneself and others, and about the ways in which people and objects can be related in an inter-subjective field of attention. Even a very young child must have some understanding that the world as experienced is similarly experienced by others and that his/her communications will, like theirs, be interpreted as expressing intentions with respect to this shared world. Such skills may sound so sophisticated that, for a child to be learning them before he or she can say a single recognizable word, may after all necessitate the postulation of a *Language Acquisition Device*. However, the work of Bruner as well as that of Trevarthen suggests that this may not be so — it is mothers who act in that capacity (Bruner, 1981).

We have not said anything about individual differences among children in our account of the four major emphases behind recent developments in the study of early language. Obviously such differences were sometimes noted and among possible causes the one most often suggested was the effect of social class. Social class, as was mentioned earlier, was also causing concern to the writers of the Newsom Report and so it now seems appropriate to return to a consideration of the educational scene in the 1960s.

Language and Society

Because linguistics seemed to have so little to offer in the early 1960s to anyone who wanted to study the role of language in learning, those working in education had to look elsewhere. Sociology seemed to offer some important insights and, within sociology, study of the process of socialization, seemed to be especially promising. Obviously families were the primary agencies of socialization, but equally obviously schools were important as later agencies in the process and in some cases there might be a mismatch of some kind between them. An immediate result of this new sociological perspective was the rapid development of what came to be called 'compensatory education'. Its proponents generally — though wrongly — assumed that such efforts were implementing the ideas of Bernstein and his associates in London, whose work had introduced the concept of 'restricted' and 'elaborated' code in language. The comforting notion that some children were failing to learn in school because they spoke a 'restricted code' — assumed to mean 'working-class' language — spread much more rapidly in educational circles than do most theoretical ideas.

Bernstein's own objections to the notion that some children from working class families are 'linguistically deprived' were eventually very fully stated in 1969 at a conference in New York. This was subsequently published in Britain as *Education Cannot Compensate for Society* in volume 3 of 'Class, Codes and Control' (Bernstein, 1971). His paper also suggests why the notion of compensatory education appealed so strongly to teachers. As he put it:

> The concept serves to direct attention away from the internal organization and educational context of the school, and focus attention on families and children ... [it implies] ... that something is lacking in the family, and so in the child ... [such children] ... become little deficit systems. If only parents were interested in the products we offer; if only they were like middle-class parents, then we could do our job.

Bernstein was not, of course, alone in his objections to the notion of compensatory education — its vogue among teachers had had the unintended but very beneficial effect of directing the attention of linguists towards language in its educational context. Nevertheless, throughout the 1960s work of that kind was widely undertaken in both Britain and the United States. Probably the best known, and certainly the most generously funded, of these schemes was 'Headstart' in the United States.

This massive programme to promote language development among 'disadvantaged' children was initiated in 1964 as part of President Johnson's 'War on Poverty'. A major component of the scheme was concerned with pre-school children and the first of these were enrolled for eight-week summer courses in various parts of the country in 1965. These courses proved very popular and in 1967 there were far more of the summer courses and also some 215,000 children taking one year courses. The first major evaluation, unfortunately, was very discouraging and it suggested that any measured gains in attainment soon faded when the children started school (Cicirelli *et al.*, 1969). One response to this was that support during the transition to school was seen to be necessary and, five years later, evaluation of a group of 6,000 children who had experienced 'Headstart' and also a 'Follow Through' programme in school suggested that positive and lasting effects were being achieved (Bronfenbrenner, 1974).

In Britain the Plowden Report (Central Advisory Council for Education, 1967) reflected a similar educational concern to compensate children who lived in areas of poor housing with restricted social amenities. These children were, it was clearly believed, disadvantaged by home-learned language habits which interfered with learning at school. These areas, the Report urged, should be designated for 'Educational Priority' in terms of resources, because 'the schools must supply a compensatory environment' (Chapter 5).

The writers of the Plowden Report clearly recognized the importance of parents in the educational process but (as the earlier comments of Bernstein suggested must happen) the Report's school-centred model of early socialization directed attention away from learning in the school context and towards the assumed shortcomings of some families. Schools were urged to establish more effective communication with parents — but the traffic envisaged was to flow only in one direction. In the words of the Report, the communication proposed would help schools to 'exercise their influence not only directly on children but also indirectly through their relationship with parents' (Chapter 3).

It is important to remember that when Bernstein published his 1971 selection of papers the first of these had originally appeared in 1958. In the Introduction, Bernstein admitted that he had unwittingly contributed to the misuse of his ideas to support compensatory language programmes because the papers were a record of his many attempts 'to come to terms with an obstinate idea which I could neither give up nor properly understand'. This obsession, in which language played a central role, was 'about people, about communities and their symbolic realizations and regulation'. But Bernstein also drew attention to an external factor which had contributed to the mis-representation. His funding body for the research project, which began in January 1963, was the Department of Education — itself deeply committed to compensatory education. They had considered the original proposal 'too academic' and insisted that the work should produce a language programme, for use with 'disadvantaged' infant school children, which would 'enhance their contextual use of speech'.

However, the socialization model, so widely misused to support the claim that certain children were disadvantaged by the language they had learned at home, could be, and soon was, stood on its head. Perhaps it was schools which disadvantaged certain children? This alternative view foregrounded differences in the power and status of those participating in the teaching/learning process and, hence, the need to examine classroom interaction in detail. The reaction was undoubtedly further provoked by some of the more outrageous claims being made about the way language was used in stereotyped 'working-class' families. In the United States similar claims were often made about 'Black English' and, no doubt, led to the polemical tone adoped by Labov (1970) in his paper on 'The logic of non-standard English', in which he argued that it is not a restricted code but the attitudes of teachers and researchers towards non-standard dialect that puts lower class children at a disadvantage. Fortunately others chose to explore what actually happens in classrooms and an early, and extremely important, example was a two-year study initiated by Barnes in 1966 which examined interaction in a number of secondary school lessons (Barnes, 1969).

Changing Educational Practice

Although linguistics and education seemed to share little common ground in the early 1960s, the situation, as we have shown, was very different by the early 1970s. This was only partly the result of developments in linguistics. Another important influence was the development of more effective in-service training and, in particular, the establishment of the Schools Council in 1964. This was both an agency for promoting research and a very effective means of dissemination because many teachers became deeply involved in language study by working with trained linguists in several major Schools Council projects. This in turn led to a deeper mutual understanding between those who specialized in language study and those whose speciality was in teaching children. The result was the emergence of publications and materials which were to have a fundamental effect on classroom practice.

An early Schools Council project, headed by Halliday, was the 'Programme for Linguistics on English Teaching'. It produced a series of valuable occasional papers, which helped to show, in detail, how linguistics can illuminate various aspects of education and then came something entirely new — suggestions and teaching materials for a linguistically based approach to the teaching of initial literacy (Mackay *et al.*, 1970). The following year a different group from the same project published some equally challenging ideas and materials for language work with older children (Doughty *et al.*, 1971).

Language use in schools was also being explored by two other London-based Schools Council projects in the early 1970s. One of these took a very wide-ranging view of all aspects of language use among primary school children (Rosen and Rosen, 1973); the other examined writing development in secondary schools (Britton *et al.*, 1975). The relationships between language and thinking was a constant theme in both of these projects and the work attracted attention among teachers in Australia, Canada and the United States as well as in Britain.

Talk in the classroom was the specific focus of another Schools Council project: 'Communication Skills in Early Childhood'. This was based in the University of Leeds and the first associated publication emphasized the importance of meaning rather than surface form in conversations between a teacher and child (Tough, 1973). The subsequent publications may have tended to suggest that it is only the teacher's definition of meaning that really matters in classroom talk, but they were very timely in their emphasis on the developmental importance of one-to-one conversation in the early years of schooling. In Birmingham, with reference to older children, attempts were being made to develop descriptive categories for analyzing the spoken interaction between teacher and pupils in more formal lessons (Sinclair and Coulthard, 1975). The work was essentially exploratory but it did begin to show how discourse analysis might be used to examine classroom talk in ways that would produce a deeper understanding of relevance and meaning than the Leeds project had achieved.

Research into language and learning was not, of course, restricted to classroom uses, and the earlier emphasis on socialization into language soon stimulated considerable interest in the way language was used in nursery classes and during initial acquisition within the family. Research into language learning in homes began at Bristol in 1972 (Wells, 1984) and in the same year Margaret Thatcher's White Paper (DES, 1972) called for a massive increase of nursery education. However, it was also soon realized that there was very little research evidence to support the claims being made about the effects of such provision — and resulting enquiries sometimes suggested that its effects on language development might need to be more closely examined (for example Tizard, 1974). Such findings may have been disconcerting but they also reflected growing sophistication in the observation and analysis of language. That, in its turn, made people in education more aware of the complex role of language in young children's learning.

The purpose of introducing these specific, though necessarily very brief, accounts of just a few of the many kinds of research and enquiry being undertaken in the early 1970s was to emphasize the background from which the Bullock Report emerged (DES, 1975). Its message may still have been new to many who worked in education but it can now be seen as a 'watershed' publication, which drew together some important research and enquiry in the language area. Furthermore, it succeeded in making a concern with language a central feature of much subsequent thinking about teaching methods and pupil performance throughout the whole range of schooling and 'across the curriculum'.

The two issues that we noted as causing educational concern in the later 1950s — unequal access to knowledge and the content of the secondary curriculum — had not gone away of course, but the writers of the Bullock Report saw the job of schools in rather different terms. The earlier emphasis on the transmission of knowledge appropriate to the needs of society, and on changing the language of certain pupils so that they could profit from what the school offered, was now replaced by a more pupil-centred view of education. Learning rather than teaching was emphasized and schools were urged to seek to meet developmental needs, foremost among these being the need to develop 'A Language for Life'.

The Bullock Report reflected a 'progressive' educational ideology but, as so often happened in the 1970s, its writers assumed that more teachers shared their vision than was, in fact, the case (Bennett *et al.*, 1976). That does not, of course, diminish the importance of the message that learning is facilitated if teachers are sensitive to the needs of individual pupils. The Report also made clear that such sensitivity demands an informed understanding of language from each member of a school staff and that all should agree to follow a consistent language policy across the curriculum.

Throughout the Report, the fundamental importance of pupil talk, at every stage of schooling, was constantly emphasized and 'exploratory talk' in group discussion was proposed as a powerful means of learning — provided classroom organization and teaching style made this possible. Planned intervention by the teacher and carefully organized group talk, it was urged, should figure prominently, because that kind of classroom talk enabled each pupil to draw on his/her full language resources when attempting to relate new knowledge to previous understanding.

Unfortunately the enthusiasm for 'progressive' ideology, which most of the Bullock Committee shared, caused them seriously to underestimate the difficulties of managing such talk in the classroom — even in primary schools not constrained by examinations. For many secondary teachers it seemed that further constraints on their methods of working, arising from pupil and parent expectations about subject knowledge as well as the examined syllabus, were virtually ignored by the Report.

In the section on 'Language in the Middle and Secondary Years' (Chapters 10 and 11), the Bullock Report argues that all teachers need to understand how talking and writing can be used to extend thinking. However, Chapter 12, unfortunately, does not make a very satisfactory case for the Committee's best known recommendation — that every school should develop a policy for 'Language across the curriculum'. One of the problems, in the chapter as in much subsequent discussion of the idea, is that it is often difficult to distinguish between the specialized concern with language that is properly part of 'English' as a subject, and that kind of understanding of the role of language in learning which should inform the work of all teachers. Developing a school language policy is not like changing a syllabus or a work scheme within a particular subject — though some head teachers seemed to think so, and hence expected all their staff to achieve a common mind about some inherently problematic matters. Foremost among the issues which tended to divide rather than unite teachers were: classroom organization and teaching style; marking and assessment procedures; and attitudes towards 'correctness' in speech and writing. A less divisive view of a policy for language across the curriculum might be that such a policy requires only that contentious issues, of the kind we have indicated, should be matters of continuing discussion for, when that is the case, the role of language in learning is also continually re-appraised.

Opinions about the Bullock Report vary widely, but one thing it clearly did not do was to satisfy those who had expected it to confirm their belief that changes in school organization and teaching methods of a 'progressive' kind were causing standards of literacy (in both reading and writing) to decline. Perhaps that is why 1975, the year the report was published, also saw the establishment of the Assessment of Performance Unit, whose task was, and still is, to devise instruments for monitoring standards, in both mathematics and English, throughout Britain. One assumes that James Callaghan's call for a 'Great Debate' on education, which he made in a speech at Ruskin College, Oxford, in 1976, was another response to the growing public anxiety about the balance that education should maintain between the needs of society on the one hand and, on the other, those of the individuals within it.

Some Issues of Continuing Concern

The issues raised in this debate are perennial ones, of course, and so it is not surprising that, ten years later, many of them are still being actively discussed. However, with the prolonged economic recession, the issue that seems to have come to dominate discussion is that of 'accountability'. The argument this issue has aroused serves to remind us that, in a democratic society, education is essentially political. This is so both in the sense of its being a major instrument for the perpetuation or the modification of the *status quo* and of its being a consumer of scarce material resources and trainer of the currently all too plentiful human resources. Amongst all the pressure groups that have jostled for position, one in particular seems to us to give cause for grave concern: this is the movement which seeks to narrow the scope of the curriculum to an almost exclusive concern with 'basic skills'.

There are few who would disagree with the concern to ensure that all pupils leave school having achieved a level of literacy and numeracy that will enable them to function effectively in contemporary society. Experience of the last twenty-five years, however, gives us little reason to believe that this will best be achieved by the imposition of a centrally planned curriculum, which emphasizes rote-learning and the drilling of skills at the expense of understanding and the search for individual relevance. Similarly, most people recognize the need for individual schools and teachers, and for the educational system as a whole, to be accountable to the wider society which, after all, provides the necessary resources. Nevertheless, it would be unfortunate if the drive for accountability were to lead to such an emphasis on norm-referenced standards of assessment that little room was left for individual initiatives by teachers and pupils or for the modification of centrally planned teaching programmes to meet the needs of local communities and of particular individuals.

Growing recognition of diversity in our schools has been one of the most important developments of the last few years. However, it was the Warnock Report (1978) that put a figure for the first time on the number of children who encounter difficulties of various kinds in learning at school: an average of one in five can be expected to experience some sort of handicap, either short or long-term, during the course of their school careers. Clearly, if the majority of these children are to be educated within the main stream, teachers need to be capable of, and encouraged to show, considerable flexibility in adapting the curriculum to the learning needs of individual pupils.

Diversity of a different kind is also to be found in the cultural backgrounds from which children come. Britain, like most other countries in the developed world, is a multi-cultural, multi-ethnic society. In their survey of London schools, Rosen and Burgess (1980) found that fifty-five different languages and twenty-four overseas-based dialects of English were represented amongst the first languages spoken by pupils. In some schools, the *majority* of pupils had a language other than English as their first language, and quite a high proportion spoke three or more languages in their everyday lives. Although such linguistic diversity is only found in large urban areas, the need to promote a positive attitude to cultural and linguistic diversity is clearly incumbent on all those working within the education service.

Linguistic diversity is also found amongst native speakers of English, of course. Although dialect differences are probably gradually disappearing as a result of improved communication as well as personal mobility and the pervasiveness of the media, regional and class-related differences of accent remain as vigorous as ever. The efforts of linguists and sociolinguists (Labov, 1970 and 1972; Trudgill, 1975) have done much to challenge the belief that some dialects and accents are inherently inferior to others, but social attitudes are much harder to change (Hymes, 1973). Yet equality of opportunity in education demands, amongst other things, that every pupil's first language, dialect or accent should be accepted and valued in its own right. To do less is to devalue the pupil who speaks it and, by implication, the cultural group from whom he or she has learned it — that is what turns linguistic difference into linguistic disadvantage.

Just as important as recognizing and valuing diversity between speakers is the encouragement of versatility within speakers. Children for whom the language of the home is not that of the wider society are in some ways at an advantage here as, with help and encouragement, they quite readily become bi- or even tri-lingual. Indeed for all speakers, even the monolingual, there is a range of varieties, or registers, that have to be mastered in order to communicate effectively in the various social situations that they are likely to encounter. Some of these varieties are acquired as part of growing up in the local community but others need to be made the subject of conscious attention at school, as has been emphasized by Halliday (1978).

Chief amongst the varieties of language that need to be fostered in school are the various registers of written language. There has probably never been a time when literacy has not figured prominently in the curriculum of primary education but, as two recent reports have emphasized, learning to read and write involves far more than being able to decode print to speech or to encode speech in writing (Southgate *et al.*, 1981; Lunzer and Gardner, 1979). For both reader and writer, the aim is to enter into a communicative relationship with another person or persons, and that means adjusting one's strategies of reading and writing to take account of different purposes and different settings.

Anyone who has ever tried to write knows that written language, in any register, requires a different selection and organization of ideas from that which would be appropriae for an oral version. Recent research is beginning to show just what these differences are and why they are necessary (Olson, 1977; Tannen, 1982). Pupils need opportunity and encouragement, both as readers and as writers, to master these different ways of organizing meaning in written language. Furthermore, time has to be found to try out these different 'voices' free from the requirement to get it right first time. There are signs that this is being recognized, particularly with respect to writing, in the widespread interest in the work of the Schools Council 'Writing across the Curriculum ' Project (Martin *et al.*, 1976), the 'Journal Dialogue Writing Project' (Staton, 1982) and the New Hampshire 'Writing Workshop' (Graves, 1983). What is clear from all this work on writing is that it takes time to do and that more than one draft may well be needed if the end result is to fulfil the writer's intentions.

Britton *et al.* (1975) make a useful distinction between 'getting it right for oneself' and 'getting it right for the reader', and Smith (1982) makes a similar distinction between 'composition' and 'transcription' in writing. Whilst recognizing that transcription is, of course, involved whenever one writes, he emphasizes the primacy of composition and suggests that getting all the details of spelling, punctuation and so on right is often best dealt with when a text is being revised or redrafted.

There are several reasons for welcoming this renewed attention to writing as composition. One is that, contrary to the prediction of those who thought that writing would disappear in the age of electronic communication, people still write in the course of their everyday lives after they have finished their formal education. Many, it seems, wish they had the opportunity and skill to do so more often (Griffiths and Wells, 1983). Secondly, because of the opportunity that writing provides for reflecting on and interrogating one's knowledge and experience, it is one of the most effective modes of developing greater understanding of the topic one is writing about. For this reason, it seems to us, pupils need more opportunity (and the necessary help) to choose their own topic and the way in which they will approach it. This is something that applies not only in English work, but in other subjects as well.

Perhaps the most important reason for welcoming a greater concern with writing, however, especially when it is treated as a mode of personal communication, is that it offers a basis for individual teaching. This naturally occurs as the teacher responds to what the pupil has written and offers feedback in the form of advice and suggestions tailored to the current state of understanding and skill of the individual pupil. This, essentially, is the purpose of the 'conferencing', which plays such a central part in the approach practised by the teachers whose work is documented by Graves (1983).

Whilst it is highly desirable that all pupils should become more proficient at reading and writing to obtain and convey information, it is important that schools should not neglect the imaginative and affective meanings that are communicated by language in both its spoken and written form. The last twenty-five years have seen an enormous increase in the range of literature written for children, from pre-schoolers to adolescents. Unfortunately, in far too many classrooms literature is ignored or treated as a sort of indulgence — to be read only when more serious business has been completed. This attitude among teachers seriously underestimates the importance of imagination.

Throughout their primary schooling, and indeed well beyond it, children need to enlarge and deepen their understanding through encounters with literature of all kinds. We believe, therefore, that regular provision should be made for private reading of self-selected books and for children to hear stories and poetry read aloud. Alongside this, of course, they also need the opportunity to explore and interpret their own experience through the creation of fictions and fantasies of their own.

Stories have always featured among the types of writing that pupils undertake in English lessons, but it is now coming to be seen that 'storying' is a much more pervasive and fundamental human activity than that limited acceptance recognizes. Rosen (1984) was one of the first to emphasize the centrality of narrative in education — whilst at the same time regretting its low status in schooling. In a recent article, he makes a strong case for 'looking at the whole school curriculum from the point of view of its narrative possibilities' (p. 19). The core of his argument is that the oral story-telling that engages so much of our shared meaning-making outside school should become an acknowledged form for making meaning inside the school as well.

Narrative as a mode of meaning-making in all subjects is certainly one way of giving real substance to the Bullock Report's call for a language policy across the curriculum. It emphasizes the crucial point that such a policy should be, first and foremost, about pupils achieving greater understanding as they use language to communicate with each other and with themselves in the process of assimilating, testing and personally reformulating the ideas, attitudes and values that are presented to them through the curriculum.

Acquiring knowledge and making it one's own necessarily

involves two kinds of interaction: interaction between the new and what is already known and interaction between the learner and the teacher. It is also increasingly being recognized that the process is greatly facilitated by interaction amongst groups of learners, as they explore a topic together, evaluating each other's suggestions and trying out alternative formulations. Where schools have adopted various forms of integrated curricula and are exploiting the possibilities made available by resource-based learning, they provide more opportunities for pupils to engage in the sort of exploratory talking and writing advocated by Barnes (1976) and Britton (1984). If such opportunities are to be used effectively, however, there is need for informed guidance by the teacher.

Whatever the method of classroom organization, it always remains true that the quality of pupil learning is strongly affected by the quality of the interaction through which that learning is mediated. In the past there has been a tendency among teachers to pay so much attention to the language of their pupils that they have neglected to examine their own. More recently, as a result of participating in research projects and in in-service courses that have encouraged them to record and analyze themselves at work, more and more teachers have come to recognize the importance of their own habitual patterns of interaction in facilitating — or impeding — their pupils' active involvement in learning.

In concluding this chapter, we wish to emphasize four recurrent themes in the chapters to follow. One has just been indicated:

— the importance of a collaborative rather than a directive style of interaction.

The others are:

— the active nature of effective learning, as children form and test hypotheses about the experiences they encounter both in and out of school;
— the value of errors, to learners as elicitors of helpful feedback and, to teachers, as a source of insight into the meanings that their pupils are making;
— the developmental thrust that adults (parents and teachers) provide when they are prepared to negotiate the shared construction of meaning.

Language is intimately bound up with all aspects of human life. Schooling, therefore, must seek to provide opportunities for children to develop their linguistic resources and to extend their use of those resources both purposefully and effectively. To do so is simultaneously one of the most important means of achieving the goals of education and a goal in its own right. The original papers we have collected in this book are intended to promote these goals amongst all those who have a responsibility for children's education.

Language and Learning:
An International Perspective

Gordon Wells

Having provided a historical perspective on some of the major issues in the field of language and learning, we come now to a consideration of some of these issues in greater detail. The first two chapters are particularly concerned with children's 'spontaneous' learning — the kind that does not depend on formal provision. The first shows how young children are helped to 'master the resource of language' in their homes, by parents who recognize the importance of their role in 'sustaining and encouraging the child's self-activated learning'. Although parents certainly vary in the extent to which they provide this support, in Western cultures the majority of children — from whatever social background — have some experience of learning through the negotiation of meaning.

In schools, it is suggested, more children might continue learning successfully if more teachers were to envisage teaching in a similar way. Responsibility for learning needs to be shared between teacher and pupil so that teaching can be collaborative rather than coercive. It is not that classrooms should be more like homes — just that, in classrooms, more use should be made of the home-like strategies of 'guidance and contingent responsiveness'.

Introduction: Opposing Views of Language and its Acquisition

If one question more than any other has preoccupied students of language during the last twenty-five years it is 'where does language come from?' Clearly, language is learned, for each child grows up to speak the language of his surrounding community. But who has the greater responsibility for what is learned and the order in which learning takes place: the child or the people in his environment? Although the controversy goes back to classical times and perhaps even further, it was given new vitality in recent years by Skinner's (1957) behaviourist account of language learning and by Chomsky's (1959) innatist response. It was they who fired the opening shots, but the battle still continues today and neither side has yet won a clear victory.

One of the main reasons that the debate has continued so vigorously is that two quite different conceptions of language are involved: on the one hand language as system and on the other language as resource (Halliday, 1978). For Chomsky and those who follow him, the central and most essential characteristic of language is its grammar — the finite system of implicitly known rules that enables a speaker or hearer to produce and understand a potentially infinite number of different sentences. To learn a language on this account is to construct a grammar — a set of complex and abstract rules, which relate meanings to sounds. Since these rules are not made available to the child either through inspection of other people's utterances or through direct instruction, the learning of them is seen as inexplicable except in terms of innately-given knowledge of the general principles underlying all human languages and a predisposition actively to construct and test hypotheses about the organization of the particular language to which the child is exposed.

However, what is missing from this first account, as those who argue for the importance of the environment point out, is any recognition of the pragmatic dimension of language — the uses to which it is put. When people interact with each other through language, the production of grammatically well-formed sentences is not an end in itself, but a means for acting in the world in order to establish relationships with others, to communicate information and to engage with them in joint activities. A child is thus born into a community of language *users* and his learning of language forms part of his socialization as a member of that community. Acquiring control of the complex patterns of his native language is, therefore, on this second account, a matter of learning how to do things with language — 'learning how to mean,' as Halliday (1975a) puts it. Through interacting with those in his environment, the child thus both acquires the resources of the language of his community and learns how to make use of those resources in order to achieve a variety of purposes in relation to different people in different situations.

Both these accounts of language acquisition recognize that children must be equipped with the ability to learn a human language (in contrast to other species, which do not seem able to do so). Both also recognize that they will only learn if they grow up in a language-using environment. Where they differ is in whether they attribute the main responsibility for what is learned to the child or to the environment. In Chomsky's view, all that is required of the environment is the provision of instances of language in use in order to trigger the innate language acquisition device (LAD). To him, the fact that all normally functioning human beings learn their native language, despite wide differences in the nature of the 'primary linguistic data' to which they are exposed, makes it clear that the input plays little part in determining the particular course that development will take. In contrast, those who stress language as resource emphasize the interactional context in which language is learned and point to the wide variation between individuals in the degree and range of skill that is eventually acquired. Because language is concerned with the communication of meanings, they argue, it is essentially collaborative in nature. It is inconceivable, therefore, that children's experience of linguistic interaction should not have some influence on their learning. How important then, is the environment, or more specifically the experience of linguistic interaction with people in that environment, in determining what the child learns and the rate at which learning takes place? Since the answer to this question has far-reaching implications for the way in which we think about language and learning in school, the major part of this paper will attempt an evaluation of the evidence bearing upon this issue which has emerged during the last quarter of a century.

The Evidence from Research

The Precursors of Language

From a strictly linguistic point of view, the learning of language does not begin until the child starts to produce recognizable words with the deliberate intention to communicate particular meanings. However, this ability does not emerge fully-formed from nowhere. Rather it is just one step in a developmental progression that starts much earlier and continues well on into adult life. 'Cracking the code' may be the most difficult part of the total process, but before the child can embark on that task he first has to discover that there is a code to be cracked. How this happens is now beginning to emerge from studies of infants in the earliest weeks of life (*cf*. Lock, 1978). From the work of Trevarthen (1979) and Stern (1977), who observed and recorded infants interacting with their mothers, it appears that, long before they are able to interact with the physical world, infants are already behaving in ways that elicit responses from their parents and are thereby gaining feedback concerning the effects of their own behaviour. What both researchers noticed was that it is the infant who typically initiates the interaction and decides when it should end. However, it is the mother who, by the timing and aptness of her responses, gives continuity to the interaction in such a way that it looks as if the pair are engaging in something very like a conversation without words.

Initially, of course, it is most unlikely that the infant's gestures or vocalizations are intended to communicate. Nevertheless, as Newson (1978) puts it:

> Whenever he is in the presence of another human being, the actions of a baby are not just being automatically reflected back to him in terms of their physical consequences. Instead, they are being processed through a subjective filter of human interpretation, according to which some, *but only some*, of his actions are judged to have coherence and relevance in human terms . . . It is thus only because mothers impute meaning to 'behaviours' elicited from infants that these eventually do come to constitute meaningful actions so far as the child himself is concerned. (p. 37).

In other words, infants come to be able to have and express communicative intentions by being treated as if they could already have them. These early interactions are almost exclusively social — establishing the interpersonal relationship between 'I' and 'You', addresser and addressee, which forms the basis of communication. But towards the middle of the first year they begin to incorporate objects and events in the world that mother and infant share and, in this way, the 'It' is added and the triangle of communication is completed. This may happen in a number of ways: through the adult following the infant's line of regard and giving him the object he appears to be interested in; by drawing the infant's attention to potentially interesting objects or events; or by marking through gesture and speech the steps in familiar sequences of activity such as feeding, bathing, dressing etc. What is important about these early experiences, it is suggested, is that, although the infant has no language yet himself, these interactional episodes provide a framework within which he can discover some of the fundamental principles upon which language in use is based — the reciprocal exchange of signals, the sequential patterning of turns, and the assumption of intentionality. Since adult speech, often ritually repetitive in form, accompanies the focal points in many of these transactions (Bruner, 1975; Ferrier, 1978), it seems reasonable to suppose that, by the later part of the first year, the child will also have formed a general hypothesis about the communicative significance of speech.

First Words

Treating speech as significant, however, is not the same thing as recognizing it to be meaningful. Perception of meaning entails the recognition that arbitrary but conventional patterns of sounds are intended, by virtue of that patterning, to bring about particular responses in the listener to aspects of the world that are shared with the speaker. To achieve this level of practical understanding, the child has to be able to:

1   analyze the situation in order to form hypotheses about the meaning intention that the speaker is expressing
2   analyze the stream of speech sounds in order to segment it into units and discover the relationships between them
3   construct hypotheses about the way in which meanings and sounds are related to each other.

Stated in this form, the task seems formidably difficult. In considering how the child sets about it, therefore, it may be helpful to consider the strategies that an archaeologist might use in attempting to decipher an inscription in an unknown language on an artefact that he has unearthed. Typically, he tries to work out, from his reconstruction of the context in which the object was found, the probable intention in producing it and, from that, the probable 'content' of the message. Armed with hypotheses of this kind, he can then attempt to interpret any regularities of patterning he can discover in the written symbols. If he can find and decipher sufficient inscriptions of this kind, he may eventually be able to reconstruct the language in which they were written. Note, however, that in the early stages of such a task the inferences are almost entirely from conjectured meaning to linguistic form. Without fairly rich hypotheses about the content of the inscription it will never be deciphered, however easy it may be to recognize repeated patterns in the symbols themselves.

The same seems to be true for young language learners. In order to crack the code, they must have some way of producing hypotheses about the meanings of utterances that are addressed to them. In considering the earlier stage of pre-verbal communication, we have already seen how the infant might form rather general hypotheses about the uses that language serves in inter-personal communication, and it does indeed seem to be this aspect of language that is first attended to. Of course, it is very difficult to know precisely what children understand at this early stage, but their own utterances give us some clues as to the sort of uses that they are aware of. Halliday (1975), for example, on the basis of a study of his own son's language development, suggests that by the second half of the second year a child has discovered that utterances may be used to communicate four very basic kinds of intention, which he characterizes as 'instrumental', 'regulatory', 'interactional' and 'personal'.

Most of the child's utterances that express these functions consist of a single word, sometimes based on an adult word, sometimes one of his own invention. In context, however, the child's parents or other caretakers can frequently infer the intention and so, if the child attempts to express such intentions, it seems reasonable to assume that similar generalized intentions are also attributed to the utterances of others. Somewhat later, on Halliday's account, three further functions are added, the 'heuristic', 'imaginative' and 'informative', the last probably not emerging until after the child has begun to produce multi-world utterances.

Although children's early utterances suggest that it is the pragmatic or interpersonal dimension of meaning that is paramount for them (Bruner, 1975; Dore, 1975; Griffiths, 1979), quite early they begin to comprehend and produce utterances that also have a referential function (McShane, 1980). Here, once again, it seems as if they may receive considerble help from the adults who interact with them. The 'naming game' is one that probably all children play with their parents or other caretakers (Brown, 1958), either in relation to real objects or, in Western cultures, in relation to representations of objects in picture books, magazines or mail order catalogues. From his studies of this particular interactional 'format', Bruner (Ninio and Bruner, 1978) concludes that the game has a repetitive and ritual character which renders the relationship between word and object salient. Equally, however, it appears that children must personally arrive at a hypothesis that there is a simple one-to-one relationship between single words and simple concepts, for otherwise how could they learn new words on the basis of a single hearing, as Carey (1978) has shown that they can and frequently do?

Rosch (1977) suggests that, in organizing and storing our experience, we tend to operate with what she calls 'prototype' examples of concepts — that is to say, with particularly clear examples. It seems likely that young children also form prototypical concepts and that these usually map quite easily on to the words that adults choose to use when talking to them. Thus, for example, 'bird' is the word most commonly used by adults to refer to all the species that most children are likely to see, and children initially respond similarly to all particular birds as instances of the same prototypical category, referring to all of them by the same word, 'bird', or by their own version of this word.

To match words to meanings in comprehending adult utterances, however, the child must also be able to identify the boundaries of the words in question in the stream of speech in which they occur. To a certain extent, this task is made easier by the fact that, in naming objects, adults frequently produce the name in isolation. However, this will not explain how the child identifies other words, such as verbs, prepositions, etc. which occur in isolation much less frequently. One clue is provided by the kinds of words that children begin to produce themselves, both at the single word stage and when they begin to put words together. In some of their early work Brown and his colleagues (Bellugi and Brown, 1964) remarked on the 'telegraphic' nature of early utterances, and suggested that the words used tended to be those that are stressed in normal speech. Children, therefore, may use word stress to help them segment the stream of speech. This point has been made again more recently by Wanner and Gleitman (1982), who point out that in stressed languages generally, it is the unstressed items that are omitted in early utterances. Stress alone cannot be sufficient, however. Although it may give global salience to particular words, it does not give unambiguous information about word boundaries (for example, 'an/orange' or 'a/norange'). To determine precisely where boundaries occur, the child must also notice how words combine with other words in the context of larger structures (for example, 'an orange', 'my orange', 'this orange' etc.). Weir's (1962) study of her child's pre-sleep monologues shows how some children systematically try out possible combinations of this kind in what looks very much like playful practice.

Gordon Wells

First Sentences

Many of the child's single-word utterances consist of words that seem to refer to objects in the environment and this, in combination with contrasts in intonation, gesture and voice quality, allows adults to interpret them in context as conveying pragmatic intentions of the kinds described by Halliday. However, if they were to remain limited to single word utterances, children would have very restricted powers of communication. For, central to language, is its capacity to express relationships, such as actor-action ('the boy ran'), object-location ('Mummy is in the kitchen'), experiencer-state experienced ('I'm hungry') and so on. These relational meanings are typically realized grammatically — by word order, suffix or inflection — and are therefore not as transparent as those meanings that are lexicalized in individual words. Furthermore, there is rarely a direct, one-to-one relationship between meaning and formal realization. It is thus much more difficult for adults to attempt to teach the meaning-form relationships ostensively, as they frequently do with the names of familiar objects.

At this stage, therefore, children are heavily dependent on their own ability to form hypotheses about meanings and the ways in which these are related to the sequential patterns of morphemes that they can identify in the stream of speech. Where might such hypotheses come from?

Quite early in the post-Chomsky period of interest in language development, Donaldson (1966) suggested that the answer might be found in the cognitive schemata that the child has by this stage already constructed about the organization of the physical and social environment. Since then, a number of other researchers have pursued this line of investigation, often using Piaget's account of cognitive development as a basis for examining the relational meanings expressed in early utterances (and therefore also assumed to be understood). Brown, for example, concluded from his analysis of his own and other researchers' data 'that the first sentences express the construction of reality which is the terminal achievement of sensori-motor intelligence' (1973, p. 200) and Edwards (1973) and Wells (1974) reached similar conclusions.

However, although the child certainly requires the cognitive schemata which have already been acquired in order to construct hypotheses about the meanings that are expressed in the speech that he hears, this is not in itself sufficient. He still has to discover which of the possible cognitive schemata are actually encoded in the language being learned and how they are organized in relation to the grammar. In a recent article summarizing developmental studies across a wide variety of languages, Slobin (1981) suggests that the method used by the child is to pay attention to what, following Rosch, he calls 'prototypical situations' — situations, that is, that are particularly salient, such as the transitive situation of an agent causing a change in the state or location of an object (for example, 'Daddy (agent) is painting (causing change of state) the door (object).') Treating these as basic semantic categories, he then looks for the 'canonical', or basic grammatical, forms in which they are encoded. Whether this or some other strategy is the one that is actually employed, it is clear that the major responsibility for carrying out the task of mapping meanings on to forms, must lie with the child. Since these relationships cannot be taught, each child must reinvent them for himself (Lock, 1980). However, it is still possible that the conversational context may facilitate the task to some degree. And during the last fifteen years or so there has been an increasing number of studies which have attempted to find out whether this is in fact the case.

Modifications in Adult Speech to Children

The first of these studies were designed to rebut Chomsky's (1964) characterization of the input as 'random and degenerate', and they were remarkably successful. Snow and Ferguson, (1977), reviewing studies by a number of researchers, showed that there is very considerable evidence that caretakers do generally adjust their speech when talking to young children and that they speak a recognizable register of baby-talk, or 'motherese' as it has been called by some, which is characterized by formal simplicity, fluent and clear delivery and high redundancy in context.

Such characteristics certainly seem likely to facilitate the learner's task, but only in a rather general way. If one wanted to argue for a more specific effect of the input it would be necessary to demonstrate that it was, in addition, 'finely tuned' to the learner's current knowledge and progressively modified to present the child with precisely the information that he needed in order to take the next step. To some extent, adults do seem to behave in this way. Newport, Gleitman and Gleitman (1977), Furrow, Nelson and Benedict (1979) and Wells (1980) have all found that the frequency with which adults addressed utterances to their children of the polar interrogative type (in which the auxiliary verb occurs in first position as in 'have you finished?') was associated with the rate at which the children learned the auxiliary verb system. Nevertheless, no other formal characteristics of adult utterances have consistently shown a similar association.

Evidence of a rather different kind, however, is provided by the Bristol Language Development study (Wells, 1984). This shows a remarkably close fit between the frequency with which particular sentence meanings, particular pronouns and particular auxiliary verbs occurred in the speech addressed to children and the order in which the items in these three systems emerged in the children's own utterances. Furthermore, the frequencies with which many of these items occurred at successive observations showed a sharp increase in the period immediately preceding the children's first recorded use of them. At first sight, therefore, it might appear that the adult input had the effect of determining the order in which the items were learned.

Nevertheless, such a conclusion would, I believe, be unwarranted. In the first place, for a fourth system investigated, that of utterance functions, the order of emergence was not significantly associated with the rank order of frequency of items in the input. On the other hand, when the effect of *complexity* was investigated, — that is to say, the relative difficulty of particular items in terms of the number of semantic and syntactic distinctions involved and the level of cognitive functioning presumed to be required to cope with them — *all* of the linguistic systems examined showed a very substantial correlation between relative *complexity* and order of emergence, with the highest correlation ($r_s = 0.95$) occurring in relation to the system of utterance functions. Complexity of what has to be learned, therefore, seems to be the main determinant of the order in which children's learning occurs rather than the relative frequency with which the items are used in the speech that is addressed to them. Secondly, since the order in which learning occurs is remarkably similar across children (Wells, 1984), it would be necessary, if the main burden of explaining this order were to be placed on the frequency characteristics of the input, to attribute something like 'omniscience' to the adults who interacted with them (Shatz, 1982). For they would not only have to know, in some sense, the order in which future learning would occur, but also be able to time the frequency with which they used particular items to anticipate the sequence of development. Although it is possible that some adults are able to do this, it seems most unlikely that all adults would be able to do so. A more plausible explanation would seem to be that the order in which learning occurs results from an interaction between learners who are pre-adapted to learn in a particular way and the relative complexity of the items in the language to which they are exposed.

The fact that, for some linguistic systems at least, there is also a close match between order of learning and input frequency can best be explained in terms of responsive behaviour by adults. As already noted, adults tend to simplify their speech in order to be comprehended by their children. They therefore tend not to use items that they find their children cannot understand. However, when an occasional use of a more difficult item to a child is responded to with apparent comprehension, they begin to use that item more frequently. And since children soon begin to produce items which they have assimilated through comprehension of the speech of others, the emergence of an item in their own speech follows shortly after an increase in the frequency with which it is addressed to them. Thus it is the cues provided by the child that lead to changes in adult behaviour rather than vice versa.

The Relative Contribution of Child and Environment

Having surveyed a selection of the evidence available in relation to the main stages of discovering and cracking the linguistic code, we are now in a position to try to evaluate the relative contributions of the child and of the environment to the achievement of this complex task. To help us in this endeavour it may be useful to recall the initial distinction made between language as system and language as resource.

Viewed from the perspective of language as system, it is difficult, as Chomsky and others have argued, to see how the environment can have anything more than an enabling function. Speech addressed to the child provides instances of language in use, but the forming and testing of hypotheses about the relationship between language and experience and about the internal organization of the language system itself can only be carried out by the learner. Clearly, if the input were to be seriously impoverished as, for example, if it contained no instances of declarative sentences, this would certainly impede or distort the child's construction of the language system. On the other hand, above a certain fairly minimal threshold, the relative frequencies of items in the input do not, in themselves, appear strongly to influence the sequence of learning.

Furthermore, since all but the most seriously handicapped children succeed in constructing their knowledge of their native language in an almost identical sequence, despite quite wide variation in the amount and quality of the input, it seems reasonable to suppose that the sequence of learning is very largely controlled by the innate structure of the learner's mind. What this structure is, however, and whether it is specific to language or more generally involved in cognitive processing, is still far from clear.

Pressure to succeed in communicating may go some way towards explaining the motivation for the self-activated learning that takes place (Bates and MacWhinney, 1982) but, beyond that, there seems to be a built-in determination to master the system for its own sake — to regard language as 'an internal problem space *per se*' (Deutsch, 1981). It is only such a conceptualization of the child as language-learner that can account for the well-known phenomenon of over-regularizations (for example, 'goed', 'mouses', etc.) and the sorts of errors in older children's speech which have been carefully documented by Bowerman (1982), or explain their imperviousness to adult attempts to correct their speech. Models provided by others are only of use when children have reached the stage of being able to assimilate them to their own developing systems.

However, if the role of the environment in relation to the learning of language as system is restricted to the provision of primary linguistic data, such a limitation is very far from being the case when one adopts the perspective of language as resource. It is only from interaction with other people in particular situations that the child can discover the appropriate ways of deploying his resources to achieve particular intentions — or indeed discover the existence of the linguistic code in the first place. Furthermore, in all these aspects of learning to be a language user, the quality of the child's interactional experience has been found to be significantly related to the rate at which learning takes place.

In the very early pre-linguistic stages, for example, Ainsworth *et al.*, (1974) showed that mothers with the greatest responsive sensitivity to their infants during the first months were the ones with the most linguistically advanced children at the end of the first year. At the stage of early vocabulary learning in the second year, too, Nelson (1973) found that rapid acquisition of the first fifty words was associated with a maternal style that was both accepting of the child's contributions and non-directive of the interaction.

By the end of the second year, when the child has already begun to construct a grammar, it is still the same sort of parental behaviour that is found to be associated with rapid progress. From the Bristol study (Barnes, Gutfreund, Satterly and Wells, 1983) comes evidence that such progress is associated with the frequency with which adults pick up and extend the meaning expressed in the child's previous utterance. Similarly, Cross (1978) found that a group of children selected because they were accelerated in their progress received a significantly greater number of sequences of adult speech which both expanded and extended their previous utterances than did a sample of children making normal progress. Even with some handicapped children, such as the deaf, it has been found that the same adult qualities of contingent responsiveness are the ones that most facilitate their linguistic development (Wood, in press).

What these findings all suggest, then, is that what is most important in the behaviour of the child's parents and other caretakers is sensitivity to his current state — his level of communicative ability and his immediate interests — and to the meaning intentions he is endeavouring to communicate; also a desire to help and encourage him to participate in the interaction. To be a careful and sympathetic listener and to respond to the meaning intended by the speaker are qualities that characterize the behaviour of conversationalists of any age, if they are genuinely concerned to achieve mutual understanding; such qualities are particularly important when interacting with a much less adept conversational partner.

In the very early stages of the child's development as a conversationalist, it is inevitable that the adult must take the major responsibility for managing the interaction (Kaye and Charney, 1980) but as Bruner (1981) remarks in his discussion of the 'Language Assistance System' (LAS):

> The first thing to note about the adult role in this system is the adult's willingness to share or even hand over control to the child once he has learned to fulfil the conditions on speech. However obvious this may seem, it is a *sine qua non* of the adult's role in the system (p. 45)

Handing over control and being prepared to negotiate meanings and purposes are the characteristics that we have also noticed among facilitating adults in the Bristol data. The following example, in which three and a half year old Jonathan is helping his mother by polishing his wardrobe demonstrates this.

J:	Do you think this is lovely?	*M:*	I think it's a bit smeary
J:	Why do you think it's bit smeary?	*M:*	Because you put far too much polish on
		**	[two words unclear]

M: Right,
Now you can put the
things back on there
—
[on the dresser]
And I'll put the
carpet-sweeper
over the room

J: Well why can't I put the carpet-sweeper over the room?

M: Because that's my job, O.K.?

J: What is my job?

M: You've done your job
You've polished the furniture
            [a little later]

J: It doesn't matter if that polish goes in your eyes does it?

M: Oh it does yes
It makes them sting

J: * [unclear]

M: It makes them sting very badly

J: Well just now some of that polish waved in my eye

M: Did it?

J: Yes

M: Do they sting?
Or did it miss?
Don't rub them with the duster darling
The duster's all dirty

J: Well how can that get out Mummy? [referring to polish]

M: Why don't you go and wipe it with the flannel in the bathroom

J: No I think I'll get it out with the towel
[goes to bathroom]
Mummy I just just have to see if I can get it out with this towel.

M: All right.

It would seem, therefore, that adults like Jonathan's mother are intuitively aware that the major responsibility for actually mastering the resource of language rests with the child rather than with themselves and that their role is essentially one of sustaining and encouraging the child's self-activated learning.

Language and Learning in Later Childhood

The emphasis so far has been on learning language rather than on learning through language. However, in practice, the two are to a very considerable degree co-extensive. Just as children learn the language system through experience of using it as a resource, so in increasing their control of the resources of language they also increase their understanding of the experiences that are encoded by those resources. The speech addressd to them not only provides evidence about the way in which the language system works but also about the world to which the system refers.

The significance of this parallelism is far-reaching for it implies that, in so far as the child's learning takes place through linguistic interaction with more mature members of his culture, the responsibility for what is learned should be shared between learner and teacher in the same kind of way that it was in the early stages of language acquisition: the child expressing an interest in some object or event and the adult sharing that interest and helping the child to take it further.

To a considerable extent this is what happens in the pre-school years at home, particularly for the children who make the most rapid progress. However, even in such homes, sustained discussion of a single topic is relatively rare and there is very little adult speech that looks like deliberate instruction. Most of the talk arises out of ongoing activity and takes on its significance from the purposes of those involved; at home, learning, like talking, is for the most part instrumental to the task in hand. As the example above shows, some of the richest opportunities for talking and learning occur when child and adult are engaged in collaborative activity, such as carrying out household tasks, like cooking or cleaning.

However, the most enriching experience of all for many children is probably the open-ended exploratory talk that arises from the reading of stories. Several investigators have noted how much more complex, semantically and syntactically, is the language that occurs in this context (Snow and Ferguson, 1977; Heath, 1983). It also has a particularly important contribution to make to the child's imaginative development (Meek, this volume). Furthermore, the frequency with which children are read to has been found to be a powerful predictor of later success at school (Wells, in press).

The following is an example of the sort of exploratory talk that can accompany the reading of a story, when the adult is willing to follow the child's lead and to share in the recreation of the world of the story as seen from the child's point of view. The story, *The Giant Jam Sandwich*, had been chosen by three year old David, who had clearly heard it before.

D: The Giant Sandwich	*M:* Who's this here on the first page?
D: The wasps	*M:* The wasps are coming Here's some more look Wow! [M. turns page]
	M: "One hot summer in Itching Down Four million wasps flew into town" [M. reads]
D: I don't like wasps . . . flying into town	*M:* Why's that?
D: Because they sting me	*M:* Do they?
D: Mm. I don't like them	*M:* They'll only sting you if they get angry If you leave them alone they won't sting you But four million would be rather a lot wouldn't it? They'd get rather in the way "They drove the picknickers away [M. reads]
D: Mm	*M:* They chased the farmers from their hay They stung Lord Swell (chuckles) on his fat bald — "

D: Pate

M: D'you know what a pate is?

D: What?

M: What d'you think it is?

D: Hair

M: Well — yes
It's where his hair
SHOULD be
It's his head — look
his BALD head
All his hair's gone

D: Where is it?

M: Well he's old so it's
dropped out
He's gone bald

D: Where's —
Is that his hat?

M: Mm ... He's running to his
hat is falling off ...
"They dived.
and hummed.
and huzzed.
and ate"   [M. reads]

D: D'they eat him?

M: (laughs) I expect they
might have tried to
I dunno
D'you think wasps eat
people?
          [M. turns page]

D: No

.3. [= three seconds pause]

D: Is that a spray to shoo
them away?
[asks about the picture]

M: Yes it's probably some
sort of insecticide ...
to get rid of them
And what's that net
for do you think?

D: It's for catching them
with

M: It doesn't seem to be
much good though
does it?

D: No they come out the
holes

M: (laughs) The holes are
too big aren't they?
And what about this
man?
What's he got?
[M. points to man in picture
who is wielding a fly swat]

D: He's — What's he got?	*M:* What's that?
D: A note What does the note say?	*M:* A note on a stick is it? Is that what you think?
D: Actually it's a sound	*M:* A what?
D: A sound What's it called on the — on the stick? What is that on — What's that man got?	*M:* Well you know um —
D: Yes . . . Sign	*M:* You think it's a sign Yes it looks very like a sign with writing on doesn't it?
D: Yes	*M:* But it isn't It's like Mummy's — um — fish slice
D: What is it?	*M:* It's a swatter He's going to hit the wasp with it
D: How d'you hit wasps with watters?	*M:* Swatters? (checking) Well they're made of plastic usually
D: Yes	*M:* And they — you bang them down See if you can squash the wasp . . . Looks very angry
D: Is he going to sting him?	*M:* Maybe he's already been stung That's why he's so cross . .5 . .[5 seconds pause]
D: Is he hurt?	*M:* It looks as if he might be He's making a funny face

The learning that takes place on such occasions is of particular significance, for not only does the discussion provide an opportunity for children to relate the characteristics and events of the imaginary world to their own first-hand experience, but it also introduces them to the potential that language has, particularly in the written mode, to create alternative 'possible worlds' through words. As Donaldson (1978) emphasizes, in order to meet the demands of formal education, the child needs to learn to disembed his thinking from the context of immediate activity and to operate upon experience, both real and hypothetical, through the medium of words alone. Stories, and the talk that arises from them, provide an important introduction to this intellectually powerful function of language.

Observation of children in their homes, then, shows that, as with the initial learning of language, the motivation to learn *through* language comes from within, as they actively seek to gain control of their environment and to make sense of their experience. Once the child can use his linguistic resources to operate on that experience, though, the contribution of other people increases enormously in importance. For it is through the power of language to symbolize 'possible worlds' that have not yet been directly experienced, that parents and, later, teachers can enable children to encounter new knowledge and skills and to make them their own.

In school, where classes consist of thirty or more children, the task is not an easy one. A teacher has to ensure that all children acquire the skills of literacy and numeracy and extend their know-ledge in the areas prescribed by the curriculum, whilst at the same time respecting the sense-making strategies that each child has already developed and recognizing the individuality of the internal model of the world that each child has already constructed and the interests he or she has developed. As in learning to talk, however, the child will be helped most effectively by teacher strategies of guidance and contin-gent responsiveness (Wood, 1983) — listening attentively in order to understand the child's meaning and then seeking to extend and develop it. This view of the teacher as essentially a facilitator of learning was strongly emphasized by Vygotsky, fifty years ago, in his discussion of the 'zone of proximal development'. As he put it. 'what the child can do today in cooperation, tomorrow he will be able to do alone' (trans. Sutton, 1977). The crucial word in that statement is 'cooperation'. A fuller understanding of the nature of linguistic interaction, whether at home or in the classroom, is leading us to recognize that, to be most effective, the relationship between teacher and learner must, at every stage of development, be collaborative. Teaching, thus seen, is not a didactic transmission of preformulated knowledge, but an attempt to negotiate shared meanings and under-standings.

Play and Paradoxes: Some Considerations of Imagination and Language

Margaret Meek

This chapter presents an account of children's playful, but nonetheless deeply serious linguistic response to experience. Young children learn their language through interaction, but that social experience does not determine what is learned. The children use the language they are learning in an active search for personal meanings and, as the previous chapter showed, they construct complex linguistic rules in doing so. This chapter show how they also learn to break these rules in order 'to redefine what counts as common sense'.

The chapter begins with a salutory reminder that it is human imagination which prevents social learning from becoming a trap involving learners in 'a game with rigid rules, unrelieved by chance or humour'. Imagination, Meek argues, is dialogic in nature and, as such, gives a special educational value to stories that capture the 'first time' feeling of early experience. Creativity and imagination, she suggests, are neither confined to a gifted minority nor something peripheral to the real business of education. These are qualities that are rooted in young children's play and it should be a fundamental concern of education to nurture them. In a period when powerful voices are calling for a movement 'back to the basics' this chapter is a timely reminder that respect for human imagination is one of those basics.

Where is Fancy Bred?

We have in mind the relation between intellect and affect. Their separation as subjects of study is a major weakness of traditional psychology since it makes thought processes appear as an autonomous flow of 'thoughts thinking themselves' segregated from the fullness of life, from the personal needs and interests, the inclinations and impulses of the thinker. (Vygotsky, 1932)

If it is the case that the development of language is 'embedded in the context of biology, cognition and social interaction' (Slobin, 1983), then we must look to the last of these to provide a framework for the description of how children find in language more than a means of getting things done or understanding how the world works. My concern is with language *beyond* its use in practical action and rational thought and behaviour, *outside* common sense as socially maintained. My theme is that alongside the development of language as an ongoing accomplishment of social life, the interactive conversation by which reality is created and sustained (Berger and Luckman, 1966), there develops the language of an alternative universe, a repertoire for disorganizing and reorganizing what counts as common sense and refined reasoning.

This essay is about the language of play, paradox and fictions, what Chukovsky (1963) calls 'intellectual effrontery'. The claim is that, without the development of these discourses in childhood within the domain of the imaginary — of unreality, dreams and stories — children would become trapped in 'an endless interchange of stylized messages, a game with rigid rules, unrelieved by chance or humour' (Bateson, 1973). Recent studies, especially those that have responded to Vygotsky's (1962) central tenets about play as 'invented at the point when the child begins to experience unrealizable tendencies' stress that the shared activities of parent and child create 'opportunities for establishing more specifically "human" qualities such as the capacity for intentionality, the perception of agency and meaning, and the child's ability to interact on the basis of rules' (Urwin, 1983). Amongst these human qualities are the capacity for fun and games, the establishing of rituals which indicate 'this is play', and the provocation of laughter, all of which dominate the kinds of activity that are indulged in for their own sake. Action maintains the feelings associated with it, so children will prolong talking or truck-pushing for the fun of it. What begins as an exercise of evolving skills becomes at the same time a structure of feelings, from joy or jubilation to frustration and pain.

In social and cognitive studies of language development, affective and imaginative aspects are not often the focus of research. Metalinguistic features are often considered but there is usually a quality of after-thought about them (for example, Cazden, 1974) and Piaget's view that feeling energizes cognitive processes, like a heating system in a green-house, is more implicitly prevalent than is generally acknowledged. There is a kind of consensus that the serious business of learning a language is something that children enjoy, but that psycholinguists and cognitive psychologists seem to have weightier matters than play in mind, even when the examples they examine are clearly extensions of feelings as well as explanations of language and the world. There is a tendency to pass over Bateson's conviction that play and paradoxes, of which language provides the best examples, are necessary for the survival of the organism since adaptation occurs by loosening up the rules for communication (Bateson, 1973).

So, if we were to foreground what has been made peripheral in language study — the emotive aspect of play — the shift of emphasis might prove enlightening. We should then remember that early lalling and babblings are outcroppings of singing and that the friskings of feet and hands that accompany lip-lyrics point to the internal well-being of the whole creature. Unlike other developmental processes, feelings in infants are full-sized, so that early communicative interactions are shot through with affect. Part of linguistic development is concerned with the capacity that language has for 'civilizing' feeling, thus bringing about an 'organized decency of the emotions' (Britton, 1970). After all, even as adults, our control is not more than skin deep and a sharp blow with a hammer on a finger or the announcement of good or bad news brings back a word, an imprecation — the earlier cry of pain or joy.

When words first emerge they are charged with the pleasure or frustration of utterance; Vygotsky's (1932) 'sum of all the psychological events aroused in our consciousness. In the young child's world no person, object or word is neutral; each interaction is charged with feeling as well as semiotic significance. So a toddler smacks a chair that impedes her unsteady path across a room, or shakes in fury the side of the cot that keeps her out of circulation, or yells the word that encapsulates her outrage: 'Orange', while the tears stream. Later, in calmer times, there can be whispers and half-sayings of words of charm, 'nice teddy', that soothe and control.

Finding a voice, according to Seamus Heaney, 'means that you can get your own feelings into your words and that your words have the feel of you about them' (Heaney, 1982). That link between children and poets in their use of language is instructive, not in the Wordsworthian sense of the child being father to the man, but in respect of 'first times', and the intuitive belief that poets and children seem to share, that words themselves have power and divination.

Words that are heard or said for the first time are remarkable to children for their particularity; their physical properties are significant. Listen to a four-year-old saying 'pavement' softly, or repeating 'a long, long time', then remember 'all that pain' in Milton, and 'never, never, never, never, never' in *King Lear*. The child *experiences* the 'first times' which the poet recreates as the shock of recognition. In the same way a conviction that language has all the efficacy of 'Open Sesame' pervades children's play because the power of their feelings is transposed into speech acts. 'Don't do that, you naughty'. is more than an adult's frustration on meeting repeated disobedience, or the ritual to accompany a smack. The 'first times' are *an encounter*, after which nothing will be quite the same because new possibilities of extending feeling-in-language open up.

Whatever else imagination may be, it involves the simultaneous experience of thought and feeling, cognition and effect. It does not always sit easily within discussion of the 'relationship' of language and mind. Perhaps we could entertain the idea that explorations and extensions of language are most powerful within those interactions that create imaginative structures? If so, the language that reflects the unified sensibility of the imagination would not be a linguistic extra, or poetic luxury, but part of the process of the development of certain kinds of understanding in both the social and intellectual domains of language use.

Arguments about the value and function of imagination often reflect the pre-occupations of those who write about it. Sartre's comments, for example, that the root of imagination is the ability to detach ourselves from our actual situations and envisage situations which are non-actual (Sartre, 1950) seems too limited an account of the relation between imagination and *desire* that is so potent a feature of childhood imagery and play. Lacan's description of a 'mirror phase' (Lacan, 1977), a period when, as children, we lack a central definition of the self and seek it in objects or actions outside ourselves, things we can identify with, seems more useful.

It also supports my earlier suggestion that children, when they least know themselves and the world, experience *how they feel* as a unifying force. As they grow and work hard to make social and intellectual sense of events their play creates 'a fictive sense of unitary selfhood' (Eagleton, 1983).

Play with Words

All children play with sounds and the evidence of Weir's (1962) pre-sleep monologues is convincing. But when she claims that 'the pleasure of play is structured so that it serves as a systematic linguistic exercise' I wonder if the opposite may not also be true; that the linguistic ordering holds and prolongs the feelings of the first encounter? If that is so, then, in his remarkable paradigmatic display, Anthony Weir would not only be practising linguistic rules, but also breaking them, because the social situation within which they were learned is absent and he can explore the boundaries of his feelings.

When my students collected pre-sleep monologues we discovered that the content and forms of the utterances were restricted, as in the Weir study, but the range of intonations stretched well beyond the tonal register of normal conversation. Variations of tone, pitch and stress were greatly exaggerated. As they practised and repeated segments of language the children seemed to respond with intent to the emotive content, pushing the tonal range ever farther as they did so. They laughed at their own jokes as they paired utterances to invent dialogues in their monologue, or played variations on a single phrase.

Play with sounds is a base for the invention of verbal novelties and the fun of topsy turveys (Chukovsky, 1963). Every family, every teacher, has a collection of new productions and linguists explain these lexical innovations by saying that children extend the meanings of words they know in order to express meanings for which they have no words. Eve Clark says children 'are learning the process required in their language for creating new words' (Clark, 1983). But if we look at the denominal verbs that form the corpus of her study we find that, not only are they strongly context-dependant, as one would expect, but they also carry a feeling surcharge of the noun from which they derive. Here are two of her examples:

'I can button it' (a child of 2.4 reaching for a pocket calculator to turn it on).

'I monstered that towel' (a child of 2.8 after roaring, with 'claws' outstretched, at a towel hanging in the bathroom).

Coinages such as 'the rain is snow-flaking', 'I'm trottering' are common in reports from adults who are intrigued by the inventiveness of young children. Such inventiveness is not only how children extend their competence to make new meanings it is also how any language renews itself — by means of *metaphor*.

Gradually the learner comes to know that there are accepted conventions for extending meaning. Then inventions are pre-empted by the more usual ways of saying things. 'I can button it' becomes 'I can turn it on' and 'I can pliers it', another of Eve Clark's examples, becomes 'I'll use the tongs to take out the spaghetti'. But the on-the-spot immediacy of the image, the 'firstness' of the perception which was expressed in the novelty of the words has gone. Eve Clark is right about the extension of meaning, but her explanation leaves out more than it accounts for.

What has been left out is illustrated by Lucy Hosegood, at two-plus, with some help from an editor (Rogers, 1979):

> That cow grey mutes afternoon
> The starlings
> On the television aerial
> Look like sultanans
> On a stalk.

The same is true of Peter Simpson's *lullaby*:

> Hush! Hush the misty music
> On the far bony hills of Japan

In these examples there is a grasping for a felt thought that would otherwise 'return to the land of shadows' (Mandelstame, in Vygotsky, 1932).

As children learn the more conventional forms of language the 'firstness' of their feelings is edited out unless it is legitimized by authors of stories and poems and by good teachers who understand the role of the imagination in the development of talk and learning. In the early years of schooling the adult listener-partner can provoke various kinds of linguistic novelty by encouraging children to explain, in their own terms, whatever is the subject of the interaction. Connie Rosen reports how a child, explaining why birds build their nests so that cats can't reach them, said: 'it's because it's too *edgery* to go along' (Rosen and Rosen, 1973). In this he was not responding to the teacher's prompting to see how clever the birds were. 'Drawing on their own experiences', says Connie Rosen, 'children see the sad vulnerability of nests, eggs and young birds.' That is what 'edgery' expresses. By making up words that express their feelings children push their imaginative construction of the total scene, of which they are themselves a part, to the boundary of their language and their understanding.

Making it Up: Sense and Nonsense

Children are continuously involved in making sense of the world long before they understand that what is 'real' or 'rational' is not pre-determined but an ongoing accomplishment of social life and social processes. From their culture they learn the language of the taken-for-granted which is locked into the many proverbial and traditional forms that somehow seem to be beyond argument. 'More haste, less speed' jostles with 'he who hesitates is lost'; 'in for a penny, in for a pound' opposes 'take care of the pence and the pounds will take care of themselves.' These older gnomic utterances that children were once expected to explicate in primary school exercises may have largely given way to jingles and slogans from television advertising but, at any time, there exists the rhetoric of realism, common forms that children learn as the tradition of certainty and absence of doubt. To learn a language is to learn what counts as common sense, and to know that 'you can't mix oil and water' does not simply refer to the engine of a car.

Alongside the language of common sense as usually acknow-ledged, its shadow in fact, is *anti-language*. This creates an alternative reality, one that is 'construed precisely to function in alternation' (Halliday, 1978). As they come to know what is 'sensible', children laugh at whatever is inappropriate, in behaviour or speech. 'Jane hit her head on the door' is a source of merriment because that is not what sensible people do. To say: 'One fine day in the middle of the night Two blind men got up to fight' is equally hilarious. But this is not a simple rearrangement of the hierarchies of common sense. It is a transgression, a breaking up of these hierarchies, in order to redefine what *counts* as common sense, behavioural and linguistic.

Long after they have learned to behave as adults expect them to, children continue to investigate the boundaries of sense and non-sense. Anti-language flourishes in the society of children as 'an unself-conscious culture' (Opie, 1959). The street and playground lore, with its seeming irreverence, its scatology, its tongue-tripping, depends much on the pleasure of rhythm and rhyme to overturn the established order of things: 'Do you want a sweet?' 'Yes' 'Suck your feet.' Rhyme is the extension of the earlier play with sounds. As they learn to handle wit and repartee, to tell jokes, to experiment with parody and impropriety, guile and authority baiting, children become wordsmiths. They create verbal rituals with a carnivalistic abandon:

I went to the pictures tomorrow
I took a front seat at the back

> I fell from the pit to the gallery
> And broke a front bone in my back. (Rosen and Steele, 1983)

Chukovsky (1963) says: 'Hardly has the child comprehended with certainty which objects go together and which do not than he begins to listen happily to verses of absurdity'. This exploration is a kind of passion; the pleasure is in the awareness that it *is* nonsense. Asking riddles before they understand the answers, playing knock-knock games as licensed tricksters are other examples. Hence the popularity with primary school children of poets like Michael Rosen and Roger McGough. Their verse catches what adults claim as sense and turn it back into the sensible nonsense that children understand because they *have* sorted things out.

Comic verse, in all its forms, is a genre by which children explore the boundaries of sense and nonsense in life and language. Nonsense and sense are part of the same pattern, as are fact and fiction. In this particular kind of intertextual language children are playing games on the edges of what is socially tolerated. Thus they discover what is congruous or fitting and also what is incongruous and ill-fitting in language and behaviour. The experimentations are laced with the risk of being misunderstood or thought to be sense-less or stupid. Long after this kind of experimental language play has stopped, there lingers, I maintain, a longing, a feeling for the glorious irresponsibility that only art, in TV or film comedy, in *Alice* or *Finnegan's Wake*, sanctions for adults. Indeed, inventive artists have become the allies of children in this area.

Narrative Play: The Structure of Discourse and Feeling

At the heart of our concern here is all that has been said about the play of young children. I have already suggested that phonological word-play is delight in utterance; that verbal invention is part of the intellectual surprise of a here-and-now discovery; that the boundaries of sense and nonsense are a linguistic playground where children explore the real and the imaginary — the way things are and the topsey turveys of language and the world. Now we need to follow Vygotsky and look at play as an imaginary situation with rules where the language of imagination becomes the language of desire (Vygotsky, 1933, in Bruner *et al.*, 1976).

We know that, by the age of 3, children are able to switch in and out of discourse positions just as they move in and out of 'real' and 'imaginary' activity. Thus they extend, in play situations, the boundaries of their world and their ways of perceiving it. Quite early they attempt in play what they might not risk in everyday activity. Their language goes with them into the domain of the imaginary, bringing into their play the many kinds of conversation that they hear in the different areas of their social interaction. In play they can say all they know in any way they like, provided they negotiate with other participants the discourse rules of the game. 'It is never *explicitly* negotiated', says Valerie Walkerdine, 'but takes place in terms of children's assertions not only of a particular discourse but also of a particular position within that discourse. (Walkerdine, 1983).

The classic studies edited by Bruner suggest that the rule structure of play, evident in the exchanges of even very young children, 'sensitizes the child to the rules of culture' (Bruner *et al.*, 1976). My contention is that the rituals of children's play, like all other rituals, sustain an affective intention — doing something to maintain the unifying effect that emotion has on perceptions and understandings. The powerful, formless, unnamed sensations that are largely present in childhood play are thus given form and significance, a local habitation and a name. Narrative play, the rituals of story-play, serve as cultural reference points in the development of what children see as 'real' and 'not real'. The diversity of narrative discourses that later become part of an understanding of cultural products called literature begins in children's deliberate play and speech rituals.

Two things come together in narrative play. First, the child's experience of an emotion in a situation which would not normally bring about that feeling — such as seeing clothes hanging on the back of a chair which became, in twilight, a fearsome beast. Fear is the response to the imagined sight, not to the clothes. The recognition 'it's only clothes' does not drive away the fear that clings to the image which is now a metaphor for the fear. The habit persists in adults. Bushes become bears and so we fear bushes. Secondly, there is the pervasive ritual of narrative, itself a game with rules.

When I wrote about young children's narrative play in 1976 I was concerned to show how extended was their discourse, and how clearly they could create plots and characters, and how the narrative form holds the experience together. I'd now like to extend my interpretation of that incident. Here it is in the original account, written with an emphasis on the children's ideas of time and place:

> Two girls, the older is four and a half, the other a year
> younger are playing on a staircase where they can be over-

heard but not interrupted. A long lasting game is directed by the older child; it is called 'Going to the cimutry' (cemetery). It is a gay affair involving much dressing up in adult clothes, including oiled (high heeled) shoes, hats, handbags, and carrying a picnic basket, dolls and a bunch of flowers. A long journey with frequent changes precedes the picnic on 'a nice stone' and a return to 'a nice tea' at home. With infinite variations the game is played over a period of three months. The scenario is extensive and allows for improvization but it clearly has an Aristotelian unity as a total figurative conception. The younger child has no image or idea of a cemetery derived from everyday life. The older child's brother died before she was born, and the weekly visit to his grave is a family ritual. For both girls it is a story game that they share, with conventions, rules, complex detail and a great deal of social talk with adult overtones. The children go about their business of processing and reprocessing experience drawn from everyday socialized living in a framework which for one is fantasy and for the other is purely imaginary. (Spencer, 1976)

The ritual of the game is pervasively important as an imaginative whole for the older child. Her brother is both there and not there. She goes with her family to 'see' (i.e. visit) him, but they never actually see him. At home, when her parents speak of the brother, they use the past tense, except when they look at his photographs. In the game he is the motive for the journey. When they play, the girls hurry because 'he wouldn't like us to be late'. The older child works imaginatively at understanding where and when her brother actually *is* in the interactions of the unvarying sequence of events. To link the game with the 'real' visits on Sundays she concentrates on the rhetoric of reality, the flowers, buses, food, clothes and weather, talking at length to her younger companion who is sometimes her friend and sometimes her daughter (i.e., herself, the mirror image). For all her perplexity about absence and loss, the game is always jolly, full of laughter.

As they refine the game the children create a narrative that is itself an icon of their feelings, a semiotic system of meanings, conversations, characterizations. The events have ritual sequences and varying duration. The play inaugurates, discusses, elaborates and promotes the imaginary and the metaphorical. The parallels are in literature: Faulkner's description of the boys' battle game in the opening paragraph of *The Unvanquished* and Proust's long account of what happened *every* Sunday at Combray as if it were *one* particular event. The children's play has elements to promote their understanding of time and reality; their joy in it is no less because they are also explaining the, as yet unnamed, feelings of loss, separation and death.

From this game we can also see the *dialogic* nature of imagination (Bakhtin, 1981). The girls create their alternative world in conversation. When they play alone children create both halves of the dialogue, speaking to their toy playmates, or engaging in *'spiel'*, a sort of sing-song recitative, 'a kind of celebration, in which fragments of past experience are caught up' (Britton, 1970). 'Spiel' is usually accompanied by rhythmical movements or even dancing. When parents notice this operatic monologue, they often say, as they do of other kinds of play, that the child 'is in a world of her own'. If however, we look closely at these monologues we find they are dialogic narratives. The 'fragments of past experience' are part of a story.

Stories and Storying

Children who listen to stories or who are read to acquire very early distinctive narrative competences which we are just beginning to appreciate. Carol Fox (1983) recorded eighty-six narrative monologues from one child between the ages of 5.0 and 6.1. She notes that:

> Most of them are invented stories, but scattered throughout are stories told from books, some utterances that Jack calls poems which he makes up, and imitations of news readings and weather forecasts. It is fortunate that Jack varies the registers in this way because he reveals clearly contrasting rule systems which he generates for different kinds of language predictions.

Carol Fox is concerned to show how children's narrative competences are influenced by the stories that are read to them: first, at a minimal or superficial level in the appearance of a character, plot incident or a phrase; next, at the level of linguistic style when the discourse is that of text rather than speech; and thirdly at the level of narrative conventions and forms, transformed by the tellers for their own narrative intentions. Her subject, Jack, returns to stories that have had a powerful impact, *Hansel and Gretel* and *The Wizard of Oz* and uses them to 'scaffold' his explorations of his view of himself.

His audience is neither the nearby adult nor another child but the 'internalized other', a Lacanian mirror image of himself. He is both the teller and the told, he asks questions of himself and triumphantly answers them in the way that narrative texts do. One reason for the effectiveness of Carol Fox's study is her ability to identify the sources of Jack's book language and its incorporation over time into his own personal narrative. Here is a snatch of the third level of development of Jack's fairy tale about rabbits, bears and wolves:

> 'then they were fast asleep but what a dream in the night — in the night they heard big steps coming along they looked out of the window they saw the big bad grey wolf...

> and we ... say ... as you know ... do you know what they had? what a dream — they heard *big bumps* coming along and they looked out of the window — um what did they see? a big fat tall heavy giant...

> They all had their supper but a strange thing happened — and — in the morning do you know what the — the boy had? The mother borned — er — borned a sister for him.

> Downstairs there was a noise, it is a noise that they have heard before — it's — it's of the big wolf carefully stepping in...'

An interesting set of parallel instances is recorded by Maureen and Hugo Crago who also kept detailed records of their daughter's responses to books they read to her from an early age. The Cragos detected in their daughter's retellings a pattern of two-way oppositions: 'good things followed by bad, doors open follow doors shut, sickness follows health quite inexorably' (Crago, 1983). The child re-invests the elements of the folk tales she remembers, just as Jack revisits his favourite stories. This is a culturally derived habit which exhibits the morphology of children's feelings when they choose either to keep or change the details of the original. The illusion sustained by the imagination is *deep* play of risk and resolution.

Studies such as these show us children involved with passionate intensity in their own world of story, something we need to know more about. It would seem that part of their pleasure is knowing that stories are 'only stories'. Hence the importance of ritual openings or 'prefaces' (French and Woll, 1981) to introduce the narrative discourse, and the coda that signals its conclusion. Narrative in play and story-telling helps to define the boundaries of the real and the unreal; it explores the paradoxical awareness of here and not here, which is part of the nature of the imaginary. Story telling both generates and controls emotions, so that the delineation of reality itself may depend on make-believe, on knowing that one can handle both the 'actual' and the 'made up'. 'The creation of an imaginary situation is not a fortuitous fact in a child's life', says Vygotsky, 'but is rather the first manifestation of the child's emancipation from situational constraints ... the essential attribute of play is a rule that has become a desire ... Play gives a child a new form for desires. It teaches how to desire by relating one's desires to a fictitious 'I' to a role in the game and its rules' (Vygotsky, *op. cit.*, 1932). In play children create the imaginative terms of their knowing. Later, they discover, in imaginative literature that they have powerful friends who can help them to extend these competences into the deep play of reading and writing.

'I See a Voice'

No one doubts that the most strenuous period of imaginative activity is that time in childhood when we play with the boundaries of our view of the world: sense and nonsense, the real and the fictive, the actual and the possible, all within the cultural domain we inhabit. We have seen how children extend their language to capture extensions of feeling and thought. Their play narrations sort out experience and language. We have glimpsed Jack at his fictive work, aware that he is telling a story while placing himself within the discourse the better to understand what he says — to become the teller and the told.

When an adult sits with a child and reads, usually when motor activity stops, children feel themselves in a different *place* once the story starts. Both adult and child focus their attention on the page, investigating the images and the words. The earliest texts are quickly learned by the child; they are often verses they already know by heart or comparable ones that they can assimilate as word play:

> Each peach pear plum
> I spy Tom Thumb
> Mother Hubbard down the cellar
> I spy Cinderella (Ahlberg, 1978.)

Very young children enjoy hearing this: they smack the page with their hands in a kind of rhythmic clapping. It is the earliest pleasure of the text. Children's first books have more pictures than text and the reader's first lesson is to 'see' the verse or the tale as an imaginative whole. Shirley Hughes, whose artistry combines skill in singling out the 'first times' of childhood, (going to nursery school or to a party, losing a favourite toy, moving house) with drawing skill in the tradition of Caldecott and Greenaway, sees a picture book as: 'a very small stage, a very intricate and detailed one to be seen close up and lingered over at leisure' because 'the best pictures a child sees are in her own head'. She also suggests that this capacity for mental imagery 'must have something to do with language and the learning of words used with relish at a very early age, even if you don't know what they mean' (Hughes, 1983).

Despite the details in studies like those of Fox and the Cragos, we are still not sure how to describe the mental imagery of children looking at picture books or its accompanying inner speech. When 3 year-olds look at Raymond Briggs' wordless picture story, *The Snowman*, there is usually an adult to direct the sequencing of events and then relate them to the child's understanding of the everyday world. Nevertheless, the conversation of the child and the adult is shaped by the imagination of the artist.

In her study of Anna's bed-time reading, Henrietta Dombey (1983) says Anna's mother 'mediates between Anna and the author by using forms Anna is familiar with, such as interaction and stress, as vehicles for familiarizing her with new syntactic forms. Through reference to shared experience she infuses the text with concrete meaning. Above all, she helps Anna to gain a pleasurable satisfaction from constructing the patterned representation of the patterned events that are the story the narrative realizes'.

Dombey's study makes it clear that the strongest voice is that of the storyteller but, as Shirley Brice Heath (1983) points out, the language of the text is made familiar 'through the routines of structured, interactional dialogue in which mother and child take turns playing a labelling game'. An American herself, Heath noted that many English children do more than label in their response to stories in school. They learn that the text can play all the word games they know: jokes, riddles, funny stories, knock-knocks and ha-ha's. The features of the oral tradition are now recaptured on the pages of hundreds of children's books as the result of enterprising publishing which offers them pleasurable aesthetic satisfaction (Dombey, 1983) in every conceivable form.

The most striking feature of Dombey's work is that it makes clear that the literary competences that come with 'the story in the book' are not confined to a minority of 'advantaged' children but can be promoted in children from widely different cultural and social situations by a skilled nursery or infant school teacher. The suggestion that children can only be read to successfully from books which offer them the written versions of their familiar speech forms is rebutted by the sales figures of *The Wizard of Oz* and the continuing popularity of fairy tales in their grandest guise.

An important effect on children of being read to comes from re-reading—it permits a re-capturing of the 'first time' feeling more than once. They like the continuation of 'surprisingness', of saying the words which bring back the feeling. As they become familiar with the beginnings of stories, so they can 'call up' the relevant discourse of the tale in the same way that Valerie Walkerdine (1983) says they do when they play together. The difference is that with a book they learn to simulate the author's discourse, the words of the absent storyteller, by calling on their play experience of turning dialogue into monologue and being both the teller and the told. Authors know that, to catch a reader, they must switch them into a compelling discourse straight away:

> The night Max wore his wolf suit and made mischief of one kind and another... (*Where the Wild Things Are*. M. Sendak)

> This is how the story begins,
> On a dark dark hill
> There was a dark dark town... (*Funny Bones*, A. and J. Ahlberg)

> Once upon a time — a long time ago — when I was a little girl, I had a sister who was littler than me. (*My Naughty Little Sister*. E. Edwards)

> Hear and attend and listen; for this befell and happened and became and was, o my Best Beloved, when animals were wild. (*The Cat who Walked by Himself*. R. Kipling.)

> There was a king who had twelve beautiful daughters. (*The Twelve Dancing Princesses*. Trad.)

The narrative rhetoric is the tune that announces: 'this is a book story.' The listener or reader recognizes the voice of a storyteller and, within the story, the listener or reader locates herself as a kind of 'dark watcher' who also co-creates the text. The author's first words state or imply 'I am telling a story for you to hear or read. This is how it goes.'

The reader has somehow to be *in* the story, in the Lacanian sense, because stories in books are both imaginative context and meaningful text; thought and feeling together. As I have already said, and as every storyteller-artist from Blake to Maurice Sendak knows, the significance of stories in books for the young is that they are both means and end. Shifting in and out of discourses is something children do from a very young age and it is no more complicated for them to do it with a written text once they have heard 'how it goes' — indeed the skill of adults when reading to children lies in being able to keep the story 'going' while explaining its relationship to what the pre-reading child already knows and understands.

My evidence of this complex response comes from two sources. First, in the kind of stories that children seem most to enjoy. They are about monsters, fabulous beasts, giants, witches, characters on the boundary of the human who, like normal adults, loom large and act unpredictably but who, within the story at least, can be tamed, made friendly and even subservient. Two modern books which make a strong appeal to children's imagination are Sendak's *Where the Wild Things Are* and Ted Hughes' *The Iron Man*. Stories like these are 'zones of proximal development' for children (Vygotsky, 1962). Sendak's words and images make claims on the child's understanding of the guilt of being a 'wild thing'. His last words, 'and it was still hot', are not only about Max's supper, but they also convey the essential emotions of childhood about guilt and forgiveness. The excitement of the story is when the Wild Things 'roared their terrible roars and gnashed their terrible teeth and rolled their terrible eyes and showed their terrible claws' and Max tamed them with 'Be still'. Then, Max and the Wild Things join in a 'Wild rumpus' together. At this point there are no words, only pictures, images for the child to confront as in a mirror. I am persuaded that the popularity of *Where the Wild Things Are* and the prevalence of hundreds of books about dinosaurs in primary schools stem from the same deep motivations that relate to the mythic properties of these beasts. Moreover, this continues throughout primary school reading and is still present in the preferences of 11 year old girls, for example, for *Dracula*.

Ted Hughes, whose explanation of the imagination is probably the best we have, says that myths and legends are 'highly detailed sketches for the possibility of understanding and reconciling' the demands of the outer and the inner worlds of imagination. 'They are an archive of draft plans' (Hughes, 1976). *The Iron Man* focuses all the images of childhood in its conflict with the man-made terrors of technology. Readers grasp its meaning as an image of 'incoherent energies' which the young so constantly feel.

The second source of evidence is in the conversations of children with artists and writers. These are rarely incorporated into research material but they are of great interest. Children write to authors more willingly than they compose for their teachers. They discuss together during Book Weeks, at exhibitions and on the occasions when artists and writers are invited to schools. Even very young children ask serious and searching questions very directly. The children assume, without the preamble that adults use to excuse themselves for seeming naive, that they and the artist or writer speak the same language and are positioned within the same discourse. 'How old is Max?' 'How did you know how to draw the Wild Things?' On these occasions one can produce the evidence for Culler's assertion that 'Both author and reader bring to the text more than a knowledge of language' (Culler, 1975).

While it is clear that children who have had experience of the 'purposes and mechanics' of literacy before they go to school profit from this experience, (Wells, 1981) it is equally evident that those who have become aware of a variety of narrative discourses, who 'possess' known texts as metaphors for deeply felt emotions and have seen their mirror image in a book, will need, when they begin to read for themselves, texts which do more than name things on a page in the style of 'This is Janet. This is John'. They will need 'artefacts which prove extremely rich when subjected to the generations of reading' (Culler *op. cit.*). Parents and teachers understand 'purposes and mechanics', but genuine authors and artists whose material is the nature of childhood, offer the possibility of interaction with texts and images that are both confirmations and risky extensions of children's early word play where nonsense and alternative language is held in suspension by the unity of thought and feeling. The effective texts say 'suppose' — that great invitation to imagine which is felt as a desire to articulate things differently, a desire that lies behind the most generative hypotheses and the most memorable poems.

Beyond Lip-service: Discourse Development after the Age of Nine

Terry Phillips

This chapter, like the next, is concerned with formal provision for learning and particularly with the kind of linguistic interaction that is encouraged in schools. Attention is focused on pupil talk in the classroom, towards which, Phillips believes, teacher attitudes changed considerably during the 1970s; and may be changing again as teachers seek a more positive teaching role in promoting their pupils' thinking through small-group discussion.

Making use of the relatively unfamiliar concepts of discourse analysis, the author argues that those who teach children in the middle years of schooling need to know how to analyze the way language is used in peer-group discussions in order to intervene more effectively and to support and extend pupil learning. He identifies five 'modes of interaction' and shows how the different discourse styles associated with each of these modes have profound implications for thinking and learning. The chapter concludes with some detailed suggestions for organizing small-group discussions.

Changing Views of Pupil Talk

During the seventies a highly significant change in attitude to children's talk occurred, a change which moved talk from something to be forbidden to something to be encouraged at all costs. As part of that change, many teachers had moved away from the dominant position at the front of the classroom, which research had shown them inhibited children's talk (Barnes, 1969), and had set up situations in which the children could talk to each other freely. By the middle of the decade they were in general agreement with the sociolinguists who suggested that the children's own language should be valued in school (Halliday, 1974; Stubbs, 1976b). As the decade finished most teachers were ready to acknowledge that children's talk was 'a good thing!' but they were not quite sure where the talking was going. In the eighties that uncertainty has become more notice-able. It is not that those who teach today are any less sensitive to the need to promote children's confidence in using talk, rather the contrary. They have, however, moved beyond the belief that it is sufficient simply to ensure that there is plenty of talk going on, and are looking for ways of promoting children's spoken language development within that framework. They want to know how they might move off the sidelines to intervene constructively in that developmental process. They are looking once again for a teaching role.

A fairly major problem for the junior/middle teacher, or the secondary teacher, who is searching for guidelines on children's spoken language development after they have passed the age of 9 is the fact that almost none exist. There are guidelines on how to set up discussions, sets of topics to be talked about, and lists of materials which will start children talking. But, with a couple of important exceptions (Wilkinson *et al.*, 1974; Barnes and Todd, 1977), there is nothing which systematically investigates what older children are capable of when talking and listening. Because most of the serious research has focused on the development of communication in neonates, pre-school, and infant/first school age children, it is to this that they must turn first.

Research into early language development, which is of necessity spoken language development, shows that adults have a very positive role to play as facilitators. It shows, for instance, that even during their first year of life children are anxious to communicate with adults, anticipating the interaction with pleasure (Bruner, 1975; Greenfield, 1980) and, perhaps even more significantly, that adults respond by adapting their own behaviour in a way which demonstrates to the child that the interaction has importance for them too (Trevarthen and Hubley, 1978). The research also shows that by engaging in real conversations, *i.e.* ones in which they genuinely want to discover the child's meaning, adults help children to develop complex speech structures (Wells, 1981) and an increasingly developed set of conver-sational strategies (French and Maclure, 1981). Taken as a whole, the research shows how sensitive adults, who are ready to listen to children carefully, to respond with interest and to be flexible in their conversational behaviour take an active and irreplaceable role in the developmental process by which young children learn to use talk for the range of functions identified by Halliday (1969 and 1975a).

By turning to the extensive literature on early language development, teachers of older children will gain some valuable insights into the role they might take in their classrooms when the circumstances permit. Unfortunately, however, the nature of schooling for children in the later primary years and in secondary schools is somewhat different from that in the early years of schooling. When children first enter school they are still learning how to learn and how to cooperate with others and to a large extent that, rather than any particular piece of factual information, is what their teachers help them learn. By the time children have moved to their next school most of them are ready to be introduced to organized bodies of knowledge in various areas of the curriculum. Whether the curriculum is integrated or classified into discrete subjects, children will have to assimilate a certain number of facts and concepts before they can make progress in understanding. When later they move to a secondary school, where the curriculum is often highly classified and therefore more difficult for certain children to relate to in any case (*cf.* Bernstein, 1971), the bodies of knowledge have become even more complex and remote from children's out-of-school interests. As a consequence of the unavoidable intrusion of more and more material, teachers are limited in the time they have available to allow the children's own conversational initiatives to develop, and in the scope they have for deviating from the topics that appear on the syllabus. They will, of course, be able to create some opportunities for free-ranging discussions, but this will never be as easy as it was for their colleagues during the early years.

Class Discussion as the Context for Development?

Society as a whole expects schools to provide children in the middle years with an introduction to organized knowledge and some understanding of the central concepts involved. Part of society also expects children to develop enquiring minds. It might be argued that given constraints upon time the most appropriate route to all three would be through well structured class discussion in which teachers first present information and then get children to explore it with them systematically. Although there would have to be a 'transmission' segment to the class discussion (*cf.* Barnes and Schemilt, 1974), this would not adversely affect either children's thinking or their language because it would be followed by a period of 'interpretation' in which the teacher uses 'open' questions to stimulate thinking and promote more complex verbal responses. This is an argument for teacher-led language development which appears at first sight to be attractive because it gives teachers a way of intervening to promote a wider variety of language functions without jeopardizing 'content'. But what probability of success does it have? For the answer we must turn once again to research into early language development.

As children are learning to use talk, they are also learning about their roles as speakers (Halliday, 1978). Adults know more than children by virtue of having lived longer so children inevitably find themselves more often cast in the role of informed than of informant. This, of itself, is no bad thing. There is often no way in which a child can find out except by getting the information from an adult. A difficulty arises, however, when this particular form of asymmetry, the asymmetry of knowledge, continues to occur over a long period and in combination with *discourse* asymmetry. It is, for instance, common practice for an adult to decide what a child means when that child uses an unfamiliar or an ambiguous word. A very young child cannot be explicit about what is meant by the one or two word utterances they use, and rely upon the adult to interpret them correctly. Although some adults are less successful than others at doing this, most are not at all bad. On the occasions when adults do misinterpret a child's meaning, however, the child is often unable to prevail long enough to make sure that his/her intended meaning is successfully communicated. The more sensitive the adults are, the longer they will spend trying to understand what the child means, but in the end, if they still do not comprehend, they will change the topic or close down the interaction altogether.

In Bloom (1970) there is an oft-quoted conversation between a mother and daughter about a sock. From her knowledge of the contexts the mother interprets the child's two-word utterance 'mommy sock' in two different ways. On both occasions the mother's interpretation is taken to be the meaning of the child's words. In a conversation reported by Woll (1978) a child at the one-word stage says 'look' to her mother who takes it to mean 'look out of the window, someone's playing music out there' and responds accordingly. The child repeats the word and the mother tries another interpretation, 'look at the fireguard'. This apparently is not the right meaning either because the child says 'look' for a third time. Her mother is very responsive and tries once more, but having made her attempt she moves the conversation on to another topic. Wells and Nicholls (1980) describe a conversation between 23 month old Mark and his mother, who like the other two adults mentioned, is a sympathetic and responsive listener. Nevertheless there is one point at which Mark's mother decided his meaning for him. When he says 'jubs (a word he often uses for birds) bread' his mother replies 'oh look ... they're eating the berries aren't they'. In some ways it is irrelevant whether Mark meant 'bread' or 'berries' for he is learning that is mother will treat what he says as meaningful and worth a serious response. In one sense, though, it does matter. If he meant 'bread' then he has learned that his mother, despite her usual willingness to listen, will sometimes decide his meanings for him.

By deliberately choosing as examples conversations in which the adult interlocutors are behaving in a manner that is both considerate and positive, I hope I have made it clear that it is not my intention to censure anyone for stepping in where children are struggling to mean. Because of the negotiativeness of their mothers, all three of the children referred to have a very good chance of coming to perceive conversation with adults as enjoyable and involving. I am arguing that extra sensitivity cannot, alone, act as a panacea for the intrinsic problems of asymmetrical talk. All children, even those who were subjected to 'good practice' in their early years, will have learned that adults are potentially authority figures with the ultimate right to sanction meanings and the ultimate right to decide when negotiation over it has come to an end (*cf.*, Speier, 1971 and 1976). Even children with favourable backgrounds will, from time to time, experience a combination of not knowing and not being in a position to make their own decisions. Whilst the children are able to engage with an adult in free-ranging one-to-one conversations this residual perception is potentially modifiable; but once they enter the context of a junior/middle or a secondary classroom, in which the adults are obliged to place fairly heavy constraints upon the children's linguistic freedom as they work in class groups, perceptions will harden. When children hear teachers using linguistic strategies such as asking 'closed' question (Barnes, 1969; Hammersley, 1977), insisting on specialized linguistic registers (Barnes, 1969 and 1976) and making evaluative follow-up moves to every answer a child gives (Sinclair and Coulthard, 1975), earlier messages about the asymmetry of their own conversational rights are confirmed. Only if it were possible to provide unlimited time for discussion and to do away with all prescribed syllabuses would it be possible to reverse this trend. But the taking of such action would imply a different view of education from the one currently held by the majority of education systems in the western world. In the absence of such dramatic action, teachers will have to find other ways of promoting children's talk development. Useful as it is for various teaching purposes, whole-class discussion is not a solution for it is subject to too many constraints to make it suitable for sustained negotiation of meaning.

Children's Perceptions of Talk with Their Peers

What now? If spontaneous spoken language development through free-ranging one-to-one adult-child conversation is not possible on a large scale once the acquisition of organized knowledge increases in importance, and if whole-class discussion is not suitable as a setting for encouraging language development, where and how are the teachers of the eighties to find a useful language teaching role? It seems strange to suggest that the place might be in peer-group talk, because it would seem that the one place where, by definition, teachers cannot intervene to promote language development is in *peer* groups. And yet there is, in children's pre- and first-school peer group conversation, evidence of the language of reasoned thinking which is so essential to children if they are to benefit from later schooling.

Before the age of 6 children can formulate simple hypotheses, for example, *Heather*: 'if we had a real one and your daddy had a real one it would be good.' (5–9 years). (McTear, 1981, p. 127), and children as young as 3½ will ask for clarification if there is a meaning they don't fully understand (Garvey, 1975). Four year olds will offer alternative suggestions if they do not agree with what their peers have said, for example,

> *Tessa*: I'll be doing the cooking .. (4) .. no we're going to
> play schools .. do you remember
> *Jacq*: yes but let's not play it today
> *Tessa*: alright we've stopped
>
> (Shields, 1980, p. 5)

and, between the ages of 3 and 5, children will seek out information using indirect requests (Dore, 1979). In other words, through their peer-group conversations, young children learn to challenge, to question, and to make suggestions of a hypothetical nature. Perhaps it is even more important though that they perceive peer group discourse as an opportunity to use language in these ways;

that it is normal to do so and the status of the interlocutors makes deference to their knowledge unnecessary, even inappropriate. Hence they learn to collaborate in order to make meaning, using their language in the range of ways that has just been described. It is not that they could not use their language in every one of these ways when in conversation with an adult; it is simply that they *do not* because they expect adults to be knowledgeable and thus less open to challenges, questions, and suggestions. Their perceptions of the linguistic options open to them in peer group interaction are different from their perceptions of the options which are offered by conversation with an adult.

When children enter the later primary stage of schooling they come equipped with a set of perceptions about what they can do with their talk in different types of interaction and with a set of skills to accomplish each type. Then, provided that they don't radically alter their basic perceptions as they get older, they should become better at using their talk in each type of situation. However, we have seen that children's perception of the asymmetry inherent in adult-child talk is likely to be actualized in their school experience. It would probably, therefore repay the time spent if we were to analyze some peer group conversations to see whether such talk is very different from teacher-led class discussion.

Understanding Intention

This seems an appropriate point at which to digress for a moment to consider a problem inherent in the study of group talk — a problem of which I first became aware whilst studying children's spoken responses to poetry. As part of that study I chose to place the children's utterances into function categories, an activity which required me to attribute particular intentions to a speaker's words. At first I perceived this as unproblematic (Phillips, 1971 and 1972) but when I compared my intuitions about speaker intention with the intuitions of other 'analysts' I began to have doubts about the reliability of intuition alone (Phillips, 1975). Two related questions framed themselves: firstly, how does a non-participant in the speech event make such distinctions? Secondly, how do those involved in the speech event make such distinctions? By applying these questions to subsequent studies of children's peer group talk, I believe it has been possible to move towards a better understanding of the way in which speakers construct meaningful discourse together.

It has been recognized for some time that there is a set of formulaic structures which actually perform actions (Searle, 1969; Austin, 1962). These formulae are given prominence at the beginning of utterances and when listeners hear them they can be in no doubt whatsoever about what the speaker intends by them. When a speaker makes a promise by saying 'I promise' or issues a warning by saying 'I warn you', it is impossible to mistake the intention. If only there were sufficient of these performative-type statements of intention the difficulties of analysis would diminish dramatically. There are scattered examples to be found in children's peer group talk, as for instance when speakers agree with each other:

> C: if we got some soft surroundings for a clay pipe that wouldn't crack or anything and that's fairly tough and you'll drill holes in that for sewerage . . . you know . . . because of the sewerage
> B: oh yeah
> C: I agree
> B: what about the fish and stuff
> E: I agree

But utterances in which speakers state their intentions as directly as this appear to be comparatively uncommon (Phillips, 1984). It is likely that this is because an uncompromising statement of intention is perceived as the prerogative of those speakers who have the authority to take control of events. Whether this is the reason or not, the taking of such power by one peer group member often creates temporary discomfort, as in the following example when one speaker took it upon herself to offer another speaker a turn which, as a peer, she was entitled to take anyway if she wished. 'G: "Barbara Barbara you have a turn". B: "er . . . um . . ."' It seems clear that, in peer group discussions, children tend to avoid saying outright what function they intend their words to perform. After examining a substantial number of classroom conversations, I have been able to discover only a handful of direct statements of agreement, and even fewer offers of turns (Phillips, 1984).

In the absence of such direct statements of intention we might assume that peer group conversationalists do not indicate their intentions linguistically at all. This is not an assumption which I now make. Left to themselves, children between 10 and 12 are perfectly capable of conducting coherent discourse which lasts for twenty minutes or more. If, during that period of time they were all trying to guess at one another's intentions, entirely unaided by any linguistic clues, the probability of communication breakdown would be extremely high. Commonsense suggests that in addition to picking up clues from speakers' intonation, facial expression, etc. and from the denotational meaning of words in the context, listeners are also scanning the conversation for *textual* information about the way in which speakers would like their words to be heard. What they are listening for, and what we as commentators must identify, are textual markers which hint at a speaker's reason for speaking. These markers may be single words, or they may be syntactic structures. They may stand alone, or they may combine together and only function as markers when they do so. To be effective, however, they must be part of a wider linguistic system; which is to say that, on the one hand, each marker must relate systematically to the others and, on the other hand, marking in general must fit systematically within the pattern of discourse as a whole. Evidence has emerged, from the study of conversations between 10 to 12 year olds working in peer groups at a range of school tasks, that sets of systematically related markers do play a large part in the establishment of sustained conversation. When I return to the main discussion I shall introduce some of these markers and consider their possible implications in terms of cognitive processes. Before doing so, however, let me conclude this digression by commenting on the relationship, as I see it, between markers and the rest of discourse.

Markers are not simply aspects of a discourse style which we can pick out afterwards but which at the time of speaking were of minimum significance. They are devices which speakers introduce to shape the discourse. Group members listen for them to see how they should understand the function of a speaker's utterance, and therefore how they should frame their own utterances in response to it. In other words, members of the group not only respond to the topic which a speaker proposes, and relate their own utterances to it topically, but they also respond to the way in which the speaker indicates the intention behind the proposition, and decide whether or not to adopt a similar mode of marking. What I am asserting is that the systematic relationship between sets of markers and discourse as a whole is one of 'organizes' rather than 'is composed of'.

The Linguistic Characteristics of Discourse Modes

I have suggested earlier that, whereas teachers of young children can promote language development very effectively by presenting the children with an interesting environment and then acting as sympathetic listeners when the children want to talk about it, teachers of older children must do this and more. The responsibility they have for teaching a specified syllabus reduces the scope for negotiation when following (or initiating) a topic for classroom conversation and it is often the case that, in closing down the range of options available as topics for discussion, teachers also reduce children's opportunities to experiment with a range of ways of talking. This means ultimately that the children will not be able to discover for themselves, as they were able to when they were younger, which strategies are most appropriate for a particular educational discourse. They will operate effectively only in non-negotiative situations, that is, in situations where a teacher takes a strong leadership role. Unfortunately this is an asymmetrical interaction in which it becomes more important to 'get it right', in terms of complying with the teacher's discourse rules, than it does to engage in higher order cognitive activity (Stubbs, 1976a; Edwards and Furlong, 1978). It may be possible for teachers of older children to remedy the situation by removing themselves from classroom interaction as much as possible, letting the children carry out discussion in small groups. But what, apart from greater freedom to range over topics, does a small group discussion offer to the children? In particular, how does it help their language development? And finally, are there any lessons to be learned from examining peer-group talk which might help teachers to invervene to some beneficial purpose, and not merely recreate the educationally negative interactional and linguistic behaviour which Barnes (1969) was the first to identify?

The first stage, in answer to those questions is to identify the different kinds of talk that happen in peer groups and then to decide what these tell us about the group members' perception of what they are doing through their talk. To this end I will outline the characteristics of five modes which I found in the talk of 10 to 12 year olds, referring to each mode in turn by the categorical label I have assigned to it. The reasons for particular labels will be made partially clear in the description of the markers and other linguistic features which comprise it, but a full explanation will have to wait until a discussion of the cognitive implications of the modes.

The first mode I have called the *Hypothetical* mode. When working in this mode, children use prefaces such as 'what about' 'how about' and 'say', and the word 'if' is used either in the same utterance or in another utterance soon afterwards. By employing phrases like these the speakers propose a period of speculative discourse in which the group as a whole contributes a number of notions to a 'think-tank' pool. As other speakers respond by using similar marking devices, or by using modalities such as 'could' and 'might', a conversation develops in which the speakers work together in a hypothetical manner. In these conversations the children are content to allow their suggestions to lie on the table as one of a number of alternatives, and they do not seek approbation for them. The following is an example from my data:

> B: *how about* things like stop watering . . . stop water your garden an' things like that . . . that'll save water
> D: *what about* clay pipes . . . what about clay pipes . . . you know . . . if you done them fairly [interrupted]

They also seem content to leave several propositions only partially clarified, even though they possess vocabularies which are more than adequate for their current purposes. A child who in one place speaks of 'vacuum', 'filter' and 'surroundings', elsewhere used imprecise modifying words such as 'fairly' and 'sort of'. In this way, they leave the finer details of the proposition vaguely defined as a way of marking their intentions. They are indicating that they are more interested in working in a hypothetical manner than they are in presenting a well-defined hypothesis which they will defend to the last:

> C: well um . . . well you could . . . um dig *a sort of tunnel* . . . *sort of thing*
> D: yeah you could dig a trench couldn't you
> E: *how about* digging . . . getting the water through a big pipeline . . . through the sea . . . and cleaning it as it goes through
> B: yeah you could have *a sort of filter thing*

The label which I have given to the second mode is *Experiential*. Like the previous mode, this one is marked with clearly identifiable prefaces. Children use utterances which begin with 'I remember' or with a similar structure which indicates that they are recalling a personal experience; or they begin with the word 'once' as a way of setting the information that follows into a time and space distanced from the here and now. As they did with 'if' in the hypothetical mode, speakers often use 'once' to follow 'I remember'. When they do this they increase its marking strength. From time to time children will check that their listeners share the same background knowledge but they do it in a way which suggests they already know the answer.

Their purpose is to show the others that they are continuing in the same mode. When children hear the words 'you know Mr X' or the equivalent, they know that they are not really being asked to supply information, but simply to nod or make a perfunctory noise so that the speaker can continue with an utterance in the experiential mode. The most powerful way a child will indicate an intention to take part in a conversation in the experiential mode, however, will be by using a well formulated anecdote. Such anecdotes usually contain some of the marking devices mentioned already, but they can also include dramatic re-enactments of the speech of one of the characters featured in them, a substantial amount of very precisely defined detail, and a coda. The three utterances below, which follow each other in the conversation from which they are extracted, show all these features:

> J: *I remember* once when we were on holiday ... and my uncle and I ... and me dad and I ... we were all walking out this fish shop and down on the floor was a five pound note ... me uncle picked it up ... he says 'I'm going to keep that' ... so he kept it and spent it
>
> K: *it reminds me of when* I found ... um ... er ... a medal in the top shelf of my cupboard with toys in and I don't remember putting it there so I thought ... went upstairs in me bedroom an' thought ... an' I remembered me dad dropped it in there ... with all the mess in there he dropped it in and it went right through the hole and I found it when I was clearing it out ... and I said 'Oh I'll get told off he might clear it out again' so I threw it back
>
> L: *once* I found a golden ring ... I think it was nine carat gold I don't know ... and I took it home to my mum an' dad and she said 'Where'd you get that from' and I said 'I found it' and she said, 'Thank you for finding my ring'

When members of a group respond to one anecdote with another, or when they respond by using any of the other markers described, they acknowledge that the focus of the discourse should be personal experience and the mode in which it should be discussed the experiential.

The next mode, the *Argumentational,* is signalled in children's utterances by the use of introductory phrases such as 'yes but' and 'yes well'. When children use one of these prefaces they show that they have registered the previous speaker's point of view but wish to adopt an alternative one. At one linguistic level, the two phrases 'yes but' and 'yes well' carry different pieces of information; the first is that the speaker is simply proceeding to an alternative point, the second that the speaker is rejecting the other person's point (*cf.*, Halliday and Hasan, 1976, p. 254). As mode markers however, both signal that the speaker wishes to engage in disputation. Children also mark their intention to 'argue' by using an assertive tag at the end of an utterance. For example, when they say 'will it' or 'don't they' after a proposition they have just put, they are being slightly more provocative than is possible when using only a preface. This may explain why such tags are less common than prefaces.

As with other modes, once several speakers have recognized the general intention to take part in an 'argument', the mode is properly developed. It might be expected that, when an argument or disputation is taking place in a classroom context, there would be some evidence of the language of logical argument using words such as 'because', 'if . . . then', 'on the other hand'. Although there are indeed a few instances of 'cos', most other such features are conspicuous by their absence. Instead, the short extract below is typical:

G: I tried that . . . . me an' Ia . . . me an' Ian tried that at
school with ordinary soap an' that didn't work out

C: *yeah well* that isn't ordinary soap in there *is it* . . . it's a
kind of special soap

M: *yeah but* we're doing different soap [froths up water]
. . . see them . . . see them holes well that's the tip of the
skin . . . where there's the skin . . . you can just see the
skin there

The fourth mode, *Operational,* is a little different from the previous three. When children are working in this mode they use deictics — or pointing words — extensively, and often refer to objects by using pronouns. Its main features can occur at any point in an utterance. For reasons which will become clear later, these features are considerably less significant as markers than the others that have been described and there is consequently no good reason why speakers should employ them in a foregrounded position at the beginning of an utterance. The high density of words like 'this', 'that', 'these', 'those', 'it', and 'them' can make the meaning of the talk impenetrable if heard out of context. The frequent use of imperatives which are not addressed to any named person have a similar effect. To counter this, children often give running commentaries — statements about something which is happening in the presence of the group and is therefore already apparent to all its members. And finally, from time to time, someone will issue an injunction that a practical activity should be temporarily suspended. Such injunctions very rarely cause anything more than a hiccough in an activity, however, suggesting that children recognize them as conventionalized markers rather than as serious instructions to stop what they are doing. The following is a typical example:

> A: push it down . . . now take that off . . . *hang on a minute* [looks puzzled]
> C: that's ridiculous . . . it's easy to light up with just a touch . . . look [leans forward to touch]
> E: 'ang on a minute . . . first of all y' just want to clip that er . . . there . . . 'ang on a sec . . . that shouldn't work for a moment

Conversation marked for the final mode is rare in my data. Where it occurs it is interpolated within stretches of talk that are predominantly in another mode. This is the mode which I have called *Expositional.*

> D: no well you see he spent it on getting presents 'cos it was the last week we were down at . . . Perranporth I think it was
> E: where was that wall . . . you know . . . where you said
> J: *along our street*
> K: what street
> J: Wingate Road
> K: at the top
> J: yeah
> D: might not have been your mum's ring . . . she might have been pretending

In this example K. has decided to ask a 'wh-' question, which he has addressed to a particular speaker, (J), whom he has identified with the word 'you'. In Western European culture, a person may not ignore a question which begins with 'where', 'what', 'who', 'which', or 'when' without appearing to be uncooperative, so J. supplies the requested information. The interesting thing about 'wh-' questions is that they set up a different form of discourse from the others I have described in that they specify the content of the following utterance. On a small number of occasions children will precede a 'wh-' question with a nomination, making it even more difficult for the addressee to avoid answering: 'C: "Gail why do roads sort of block up" G: "there's a trillion cars parked on the side of the road."' The children studied appeared reluctant to use language in the expositional mode for more than the briefest stretches of time, perhaps recognizing strong similarities between it and the discourse mode most often used when a teacher is present — *cf.*, Sinclair and Coulthard (1975) who identify 'elicitations' and 'nominations' in classroom talk.

It would be foolish to suggest that the particular language items used by these children to create each mode are the only ones which they could so use. There is, of course, no one-to-one correspondence between specific words and a speaker's intention. What there does appear to be, however, is a range of items which members of a particular speech community accept as significant indicators of that intention. When listeners hear a speaker use an item from that set, they recognize it as a tentative proposal for operating in a certain mode and they often respond in a manner which acknowledges the proposal. Amongst these 10 to 12 year olds there is a readiness to make responses compatible with previous utterances (although not necessarily *immediately* preceding ones) as in the following example:

> B: *what about* a bucket shaped roof ... a bucket shaped roof ... the rain falls in it and then it goes into your systems an' that
> E: you have sort of an automatic [interrupted]
> P: you have to clean the water
> R: yer don't
> P: you do
> A: yer do
> C: feel it
> E: *what about if* you have sort of an automatic fing what senses dirt. um if water i ... s [drawn out] clean or dirty and you have two different um ...

A consequence of this collaborative behaviour is that there are many times during the discussions when the children produce conversation which has a distinctive and cohesive style. Because of what seems to be a highly developed ability to communicate indirectly their preference for a particular way of conversing, 10 to 12 year olds working in peer-groups are able to organize their conversation cohesively without it ever becoming necessary for any individual to take charge, either by *dictating* an agenda or by *prescribing* the language and the discourse strategies to be used. Through no fault of their own, teachers are rarely able to adopt the same strategies; nor indeed does it automatically follow that they should attempt to do so, for we have not yet answered the question, 'what are the implications for teacher intervention?'

Discourse Styles and Mental Processes

The data quoted has shown that, in peer group conversations associated with school tasks, 10 to 12 year olds are liable to adopt one of five discourse styles, after signalling their individual preferences in mode-marked language. The five styles are the Hypothetical, the Experiential, the Argumentational, the Operational and the Expositional, and each derives from a similarly named mode. An utterance in a particular mode is, in effect, a bid for the associated style. The children studied successfully constructed in any one conversation a series of sequences in particular styles and, when I examined the various sequences, I found that the style of each was closely related to a different sort of mental activity. Each style offered the children *some* opportunity to develop thinking but, not all provided a framework within which educationally valued higher order cognitive activity was facilitated. That is why it is salutory for teachers to compare their intuitive assumptions about classroom talk and children's thinking with the evidence of what is actually taking place. To do so may help one to decide when and how to intervene.

In many later primary and secondary classrooms teachers are happy to allow children to talk whilst they are working on a practical activity and some expect the children to indulge in what they call 'social chit-chat'. They do not take exception to this because they hold with the popular view that, in general, if children are talking whilst engaged in practical work the learning process is being facilitated. Second only to teacher-led class talk, talking whilst doing something practical is the most common form of school talk, judging by the fact that this is what many teachers have in mind when they report that there is peer group talk in their lessons. In the light of this it is worth looking again at the style which predominated in the conversation of two groups of children who were trying to repair an electric circuit. The style was operational, and lest it be said that practical activity *must* lead to an operational style, I would like to re-iterate the view which informs my whole argument, namely that children negotiate together to arrive at a way of talking and are therefore not constrained to produce any one style more than any other. When they do choose to work in an operational style, however, this has an immediate effect upon the nature of their cognitive activity.

In the operational mode speakers make a large number of references to objects which they are at that moment manipulating or on which they intend someone else in the group to carry out some action. They do not use the name of the object but refer to it in ways which turn listeners' attention towards it, quite literally. Neither do they name people who are to be responsible for the action. Interpersonally this is a sensible strategy as it avoids the problems which arise from the assumption of too much power by individuals. However, what it also leads to is a kind of 'decision-making in action.' The videotapes show that several children move forward in response, one reaches the object of attention first, and the others withdraw. In effect, what language in the operational mode does is to turn the children's attention outwards to the context and to encourage action rather than thoughtful discussion. Only if a request to turn away from the action and 'think' is made successfully will this change. In my tapes, however, there is no evidence of this happening. The nearest that anyone comes to sharing their thoughts with their peers is when they make a commentary on what is happening. This does not mean that individuals in the group are not thinking about the problems, possibilities, and probable outcomes of certain actions; it does mean, though, that they are not sharing any of their thoughts. It seems highly likely, therefore, that the operational mode discourages long-term planning and reflective thought.

Although to my knowledge there has been no serious study of the styles of spoken language which are most common in post-infant classrooms, informal observations by myself and others with regular access to classes of older children suggest that, after the operational, the next most used peer-group style is the argumentational. If children are asked to get into groups to discuss an issue and reach a decision, one of the possibilities is that their language will develop this style. Hoping to encourage children to think for themselves, a teacher may choose an issue which derives from the syllabus and ask them to come up with a set of views on it. This is one obvious way of removing the teacher from the centre-stage of class discussion and is therefore favoured by those who are aware of some of the less desirable effects of teacher intervention. But when an argumentational style is adopted what are the cognitive outcomes and how closely do they approximate to those that teachers are looking for?

Contrary to many people's expectations, children engaged in an educational argument seem to be oriented in favour of co-operativeness. The fact that they attempt to avoid taking on a dominant role indicates this, and hence makes me a little wary of using the terminology of conflict employed by otherwise highly insightful commentators on small group talk (*cf.*, Barnes and Todd, 1977). This cooperative orientation is reflected in the choice of prefaces, which serve tactfully to put to one side a previous speaker's suggestion without making it obvious. Speakers give a verbal nod in the direction of the previous speaker and then present their own opinion. The willingness to co-operate does not hide the fact that speakers are preoccupied with their own views, however, because we not only see them dismissing other opinions, but we also notice that they confine the use of words like 'cos' to attempts to justify their own position, and refrain from using them to explain why they have rejected the proferred alternatives. When this is combined with the propensity for reinforcing their own statements with tags like 'will it' and 'don't they', we have a discourse style which asserts rather than argues. It follows that the argumentational discourse practised by 10 to 12 year olds does support thoughtful activity, especially when the children feel they must defend an opinion, but it does not lead to a public consideration of the reasoning processes by which speakers select one suggestion rather than any of the alternatives. The children do not seem to be aware that they could delay a decision to 'reject' a proposition until they have considered its pros and cons and reasoned them through in open discussion.

There is very little expositional discourse in the talk of 10 to 12 year olds as they work in peer groups, and consequently I will not devote much space to it here. It is significant only because it is the style of discourse used most often by teachers and pupils in whole class discussions (Sinclair and Coulthard, 1975; Coulthard and Montgomery, 1981; Barnes, 1976). It is the least negotiable form of discourse, irrespective of the authority or status of the people who use it, because a question addressed to a named individual demands of that individual two things. First, that he/she should take the next discourse turn (in other forms of discourse people are not obliged to speak unless they feel they have something to say), and secondly, that the subject matter of the response should be exactly and precisely the one defined by the questioner. The question-answer sequence organizes talk in two-part exchanges, focusing attention on what has just been said instead of encouraging listeners to scan across larger stretches of the discourse. In that respect it actually *dis*courages the non-questioned from engaging in reflective thought and from making explicit their considered reasoning.

What, then, of the remaining styles, the hypothetical and the experiential? How do they differ from the other three, and what is the significance of these differences for the development of thinking? The major difference is in the way the language that is used directs participants' attention. Both oblige group members to review the conversation itself; to treat the text as a shared field and to treat remarks made at any point as remaining present for contemplation during an extended period of time. When children ask 'what about if . . .' or 'how about . . .' they are signalling that they do not require an immediate response with a definitive answer; that they are seeking other ideas to lie on the table with their own. When they use 'could', 'might' etc. they are encouraging each other to consider a possibility, and to look at that possibility alongside all the others that have been brought up earlier in the conversation. And when they begin with 'I remember . . .' or recount an anecdote starting 'once when . . .', or enquire 'you know so and so . . .', they are saying to each other something like 'please treat the words that follow as something to be shared and savoured and contemplated' (*cf.,* Applebee, 1978). At those points where hypothetical or experiential style talk is developed and sustained, a framework is provided which encourages children to turn away from the immediate and to reflect, hypothesize, evaluate, and order. They are encouraged, in fact, to become actively involved in their own learning.

Teaching, Talking and Learning

Teachers of older children sometimes feel guilty because they are not able successfully to adopt the more enlightened practices of their first school colleagues. Although they realize that extensive use of class discussion can have a negative effect upon the children's language if they employ mainly closed questions, they find it difficult to teach without using them. They are aware that they talk twice as much as all the children put together (Bellack *et al.,* 1966), but they also know that you can't hold a discussion with twenty or more children without exercising some leadership. Perhaps that is why, in the seventies, many teachers, responded to the call to give talk greater recognition by 'permitting' children to chatter whilst they worked, and by encouraging them to discuss things in small groups. Ironically, however, the increase in the quantity of talk in school turned attention away from a consideration of the overall *quality* of the talk, especially its appropriateness for particular educational purposes. It was almost as if such teachers believed that talk *per se* would promote the range of cognitive processes demanded of children as they moved towards and through secondary schooling.

In the eighties there has been a reaction and many more teachers have reverted totally to class teaching because, as they put it, 'at least you know where you're going' and 'it's the simplest way to teach the basics'. The frustrations of trying to cope with the nearly impossible have become too much for them and, rather than merely pay lip service to the idea of children learning through undifferentiated group talk, they have opted for the simple alternative. At a time when research has shown that there is a range of writing styles, within which one style is more appropriate for a particular function than another (Britton, 1971; Wilkinson *et al.*, 1979; Bereiter, this volume), there is a trend towards paring back the range of options for talk. But, as I hope I have shown, there are probably as many styles of talking as there are styles of writing, each one fostering a different kind of cognitive process. So what might teachers do instead of going 'back to the basics'? How might they take children 'forward to fundamentals' in terms of such fundamental life-skills as: (a) being able to argue in a way which is rational and does not confuse the argument with its proponent; (b) being able to reflect upon and evaluate ideas and experiences; and (c) being able to adopt a style of language which is appropriate for the purpose it is intended to serve?

It is always easier to give advice than it is to put it into practice, and I do not pretend that it is a simple matter to implement policies for the development of spoken language in the post first school period. Nevertheless I offer some suggestions in the hope that any discussion which arises from them will prove valuable as a first step.

Secondary English teachers, primary teachers with posts of special responsibility for language and researchers must get together as quickly as possible to establish a clearer picture of older children's talk. There is extensive information available from research into the early years of language development, but very little to help our understanding of what occurs in later years. Until we have that information we shall continue to be nervous, even suspicious, of any talk which deviates from the pattern we know most about — class 'discussion' in other words. We urgently need to be able to handle the assessment of performance instruments being developed by the APU in Britain and by the State-government sponsored equivalents in North America and Australia. And I use 'handle' in the sense of criticize, supplement, and adapt. Clearly, not all that is in these tests will be antithetical to a developmental view of spoken language but, unless we have a firmly based understanding of what that development looks like, we shall be in no position to judge what is of value in the materials and what is not. We have to know where the children's language is likely to be going.

The other points I have to make are much less hortatory, and are concerned with action at the classroom level. A curriculum which brings children more and more into contact with organized bodies of knowledge demands that we use the school day efficiently. If we aim to facilitate spoken language development and, with it, cognitive processes, we must be selective about the kinds of conversation we encourage; and we must also structure the talk. I don't mean that we should prescribe rules for this kind of talk or that kind of talk, only that we should take account of what is known about styles of discourse and their relationship to children's thinking, and that we should develop routines which will help the talk, where appropriate, to be an instrument for higher order cognitive activity. In view of what has been said about the mode of talk that accompanies much practical activity, for instance, it would seem worthwhile to organize the activity so that there is a planning stage when discussion takes place away from the materials to be used, then an activity stage, followed by a withdrawal for further discussion in which group members can reconsider their initial ideas and fashion modified ones, then a second activity stage, and a final report back stage. It would not be too difficult to establish such a routine for practical activities right across the curriculum, activities such as solving a mathematical problem, constructing a model or designing a layout, or carrying out a scientific experiment. The biggest advantage of such a procedure would be that it would accustom children to the fact that they can interrupt the flow of operational language at any point to do some thinking. In time it might be possible to draw the children's attention to what has been happening, and then invite them to interrupt, themselves, when they perceive the moment to be right.

To take a second example — in this case the language of argument/discussion — it might be beneficial to frame discussion topics in ways which invite speculation and leave conclusions open, instead of requiring children to reach a decision. The kind of topic which involves selecting what to include and what to exclude from a list would then be a first stage, to be followed by a discussion in which children make explicit the reasons for their selection. At that stage of development they can be encouraged to explain why they are rejecting someone else's suggestion before they give reasons for their own.

If, throughout the middle years, children are encouraged to listen to as many different models of spoken language as possible, at the secondary stage they will be ready to work out, with their teachers, *how* speakers achieve their purposes. Taped interviews, radio and television broadcasts, and film are excellent sources for such studies. In media studies it has been realized for quite a while that it is important to study the visual component of such materials and it could only be beneficial to give prominence also to the study of the spoken text.

It would be possible to continue with a list of 'for instances' for a long time, but I shall conclude by drawing out the main principles upon which they were formulated. Spontaneous spoken language development does not stop the moment a child leaves the first school, but the nature of later schooling means that we cannot rely on there being sufficient opportunity for spontaneous classroom conversation to guarantee that the development which does occur will be adequate for a wide range of educational purposes. Teachers have to be ready to structure opportunities for talk in a way which takes cognizance of the fact that different styles of talk are suited to different forms of mental activity.

It should not be forgotten, however, that real conversation is not a series of isolated exchanges but a cumulative process in which meaning is jointly constructed. (*cf.*, Coulthard and Brazil, 1979; Berry, 1980). It would be a retrograde step, therefore, if structuring were to be equated with teacher prescription of ways of talking. This would be to ignore what we know about children's competence in 'doing it themselves'. To be in the best interests of children the structure will have to be one in which talk is presented as being capable of performing a range of functions. In the later primary years this will probably mean the establishment of classroom routines which make it clear that a particular activity can be talked about in several different ways, each one of which is appropriate to a specific outcome.

Children must move toward becoming autonomous learners and, in order to achieve such autonomy they must first be given opportunities to try out their language in a wide range of contexts. They can then be invited to reflect upon how successful they have been, how they might do it differently next time, and why. The teacher intervention consists of making sure that this post-discussion reflection on the way of talking does take place, so that the children can make their own decisions about possible changes in their linguistic behaviour. During the secondary stage it should then become possible to formalize a description of discourse styles, drawing on what the children have learned earlier by using talk and reflecting informally upon it. At that stage it may be appropriate to discuss with them the connection between styles of discourse and forms of cognitive activity. After all, by the time pupils have arrived at that point in their schooling, we expect them to take on at least some complex modes of thought and cope with them in appropriate language. It is true that, more often, they will be required to do this in writing but it seems likely that, if they are able to do it consciously in talk, it will come more easily to them in writing.

Which brings me to my final point. Teachers expect to help children to see how they can develop their written language and are ready to examine written texts — the children's own writing, stories, poems, newspaper articles, etc. — in order to do so. Spoken language forms a text, too, and with current technology it is possible to capture these texts and study them. If we are to do more than pay lip-service to the need to develop children's spoken language after they leave their first school, we need to make a serious study of their spoken texts.

Notes on the Transcripts

The transcript extracts are all taken from peer-group discussions arising out of ongoing class activities. In each case the broad topic had been introduced by the class teachers on an earlier occasion when it became relevant to either the Science, Environmental Studies, or English curriculum they were teaching. The sub-topic on which the children focused in their small groups grew spontaneously from the original topic but was not necessarily one the teacher had in mind. It may assist understanding of the extracts to know the particular topic to which it refers and to be aware of the starting point.

1 p. 66 : p. 69 (i) and (ii). The original topic was 'water resources'. It arose during a long dry spell when water use was restricted by local authority edict. The children had chosen to explore ways of circumventing local byelaws by finding alternative methods of bringing water to the newly built but as yet unoccupied row of houses opposite their school.

2 p. 70 and p. 72 (ii). The children were presented with three poems to read together. The teacher chose the poems, but the children selected the one about 'finding thing' for their small group discussion.

3 p. 71. The teacher introduced the notion of 'surface tension' as part of a series of science lessons. The children are trying to put together a list of small objects which float and are attempting to explain why.

4   p. 72 (i). The week before the recording the teacher had introduced the topic of 'electricity' and there had been some general class discussion. On this occasion the group is trying to discover why the simple electric circuit they have in front of them will not work.

5   p. 73. These children live in a seaside town where holidaymakers have left unwelcome litter and their teacher has used this fact to introduce the topic of 'pollution'. Several days after the topic was first broached the group decided that the local water supply was probably unclean because of the rubbish dumped in it and were exploring ways of collecting pure water.

Language and Learning in Multi-Ethnic Classrooms: Strategies for Supporting Bilingual Students

Silvaine Wiles

In this chapter, as in the last, the emphasis is on what recent research suggests should happen in classrooms. Furthermore, it is an important reminder that English is not the only language to be considered when discussing language and learning in British schools. We live in a multi-ethnic society and, among other things, that requires a positive attitude towards bilingualism. Wiles has no doubt that 'activities that are good for second language learners are also good for all students'. Like Phillips, she is also concerned to emphasize the importance of peer-group talk when it is carefully managed by the teacher.

This chapter raises a number of contentious issues, not least being the question of teaching some or all of the curriculum to very young children in their mother tongue. As Wiles makes clear, discussion of this important issue might often be more useful if it were more widely understood that 'the development of linguistic concepts per se is central to children's overall intellectual and academic development' and that these can be acquired more effectively in the mother tongue than in an, as yet, imperfectly understood second language. A serious exploration of the questions posed at the end of this chapter should do much to ensure that the needs of a very large number of pupils are satisfactorily met.

The Situation of Bilingual Children in Our Schools

In most parts of the world people become bilingual, or indeed multilingual, as a natural part of growing up or of living in a situation where it is considered a normal state of affairs — simply part of being alive. Yet setting out consciously to learn a second language is seen in some countries, Britain being a very clear example, as difficult, something to be reserved only for the most academic of our children and, it has to be admitted something we're not even very good at.

But today there are many areas of England and Wales where a high percentage of students use two or more languages in a wide range of activities in their daily lives. The findings of the Linguistic Minorities Project, in their Schools Language Survey, showed that, in the five English LEAs that they surveyed, from 7 per cent to 30 per cent of the children reported spoken skills in a minority language and 40 per cent to 50 per cent of those pupils also reported some literacy skills in a minority language (LMP/LINC, 1983). Another 1983 survey found that 147 different languages were represented in Inner London schools and one in six children spoke English as a second language (ILEA, 1983).

These facts sit unhappily with earlier attitudes to bilingualism, which were on the whole negative (Macnamara, 1966). Today educators are much more likely to see bilingualism as a resource (although those in charge of the purse strings don't always act as though they really believe this to be the case). The older notions of bilingualism as a handicap still surface from time to time, however, as the recent preoccupation with semilingualism proves. That earlier, negative, attitude to bilingualism meant that such pupils were often placed at a definite disadvantage, academically and culturally. Approaches to teaching them English, whether as a second or foreign language, were rigid, with much emphasis on drilling, repetition and getting it right, rather than on encouraging the notion that it was communication that was paramount. In fact, earlier attitudes to developing the first language were not so very dissimilar, and the approach to teaching a second language can be seen as having been influenced by generally held views about language acquisition and development that were quite inadequate. One still comes across children being taught English as a second language through a series of barely disguised drills (practising the present continuous or past tense perhaps) but then Ronald Ridout has provided countless similar exercises for native speakers of English. They are all equally ineffective and equally good at switching the children off, and teachers go on wondering why there is so little carry over when it comes to 'real' language situations.

Contrary to recent popular opinion, supporting children's first language will not be detrimental to their learning of a second. Recent research shows that a well-developed first language has spin-offs for the second language (Cummins, 1982; Saunders, 1982). It is language development in general that is important; the particular language through which this is mediated is less important. The Bradford MOTET (Mother Tongue and English Teaching) project showed this clearly. Punjabi speakers who were taught half the time in Punjabi and half in English in the reception class did better than Punjabi speakers taught full-time in English over the period of a year. Not surprisingly, their development in Punjabi was better, but so was their English. And of course they settled into school much better, were happier and learnt to answer back more rapidly.

Some Implications for Classroom Practice

Recent research is pointing us in new directions. Happily, not only our impoverished views of language are being challenged but the newer approaches to language development also mesh in better with the view of children as active participants in their own learning (rather than empty vessels) and as having many resources which they bring to the learning situation and on which we can build. Research findings suggest that when learning a second language (and there are many similarities with first language acquisition) the following are important considerations:

1 The Need to Communicate

Although in this country we tend to think that only the academically able are capable of learning a second/foreign language, research has never shown a direct link between IQ and the ability to speak another language well (Darcy, 1963; Peal and Lambert, 1962). The really important dimension seems to be motivation. If one really wants or needs to learn another language, it can be done. Traders who move from one country to another, for example, quickly learn to speak the local language, as their livelihood depends on it. Bilingual children in this country are on the whole highly motivated to learn English as they recognize that they need it in order to survive and, hopefully, thrive (see for example, Hester, 1982).

Silvaine Wiles

2   The Importance of Listening Time

Before they start to speak, children learning their first language spend approximately a year as active listeners, tuning in to the sounds of the language around them, learning to respond to different intonation patterns, gradually and tentatively trying out individual sounds, then groups of sounds, then the first words (Lenneberg, 1966). It is not being suggested that second language learners will also need to listen for as long as this before starting to speak. They have already learnt a language and know a lot about how language works and won't for example need to build up from sounds to words. But they do need to hear lots of examples of the language being used so that they can start to construct their own model of the language (Nord, 1980).

3   Insisting on Oral Responses Too Early May Hinder
  Learning

We shouldn't worry too much if, initially, the child doesn't wish to participate. This is true if we are thinking either of oral participation or of participation generally in the life of the class. Not only is listening time important, looking time is important too. Young children joining a nursery or reception class will spend a very long time on one activity, using this as an 'excuse' to look around and see what the form is in other parts of the classroom before finding the confidence to sally forth and try something else. (Standing 'painting' at the easel is a good activity, as you can remain largely hidden while you carefully scan for potential friends and interesting activities.) Children new to the class need time to scan and absorb the routines before being expected to participate enthusiastically and confidently (Ministry of Education, British Columbia, 1979).

Silence is a powerful weapon. In normal communication situations we require some sort of response from our listeners — a nod, a sound of encouragement ('mmm ... yes ...') to show that the person is still listening/following what we are saying, or even a snort of suprise/disagreement/indignation etc. Faced with total silence, most normal people will dry up fairly quickly. And then there's the teacher's need for reassurance. Am I doing the right thing? Is the child learning anything? We need constantly to remind ourselves that it may be unrealistic to expect a response in the early stages and that we shouldn't feel inadequate or threatened by this. The child will almost certainly be learning a lot: comprehension is always well ahead of production. Think of yourself in a foreign language situation: you probably understand far more than you can say. If the child, to please the teacher, is struggling to make some kind of response, the effort to produce language may get in the way of understanding what is being said.

Some years ago a small piece of research carried out with a class of adults learning English as a foreign language showed that those who kept quiet and didn't respond to the teacher's constant pressure for 'answers' actually learnt faster and more efficiently. Among other things, they no doubt benefited from hearing the teacher 'correct' the keen responders, without suffering the full glare of the teacher's undivided attention. In the literature there are even cases of people learning a language only through listening to it spoken.

However, our long term aim is undoubtedly to have all children participating fully in the communication of the classroom. Some early stage learners of English will be using their few words of English creatively within the first couple of weeks, others may not venture a word for anything up to a year or more. This is quite normal and one will no doubt be reassured by observing a growing level of comprehension and a greater readiness to engage in peer-group, if not teacher/child, communication. If one is still worried, it is always possible to take steps to find out what the child's command of his/her first language is like. But, above all, he/she must be given time (Nord, 1980).

4   Children Make Excellent Teachers and Helpers

Peer-reinforced language development is one of the strongest motivators for language learning. Because peer group talk is so important for children's language development (first and second) it is essential that we organize our classroom learning to take account of this. If we are lucky enough to eavesdrop on the extended discussions children have with each other, we cannot fail to be impressed by their linguistic range (much of which we are not aware of in the more formal adult/child exchanges) and the extent to which they support each other. There are many instances in our recordings of children helping each other; suggesting the 'right' word, modelling whole sentences for bilingual children, even differentiating the help they give to classmates reading together according to the reading ability of the individual child (Wiles, 1979). Children frequently understand the learning blocks experienced by peers, having only recently passed that way themselves. Collaborative, small-group learning is of great benefit to second language learners but it needs to be structured and nurtured by the teacher. In practice, this is not widely encouraged as a method of learning in school and may be viewed by children as cheating in the context of other teaching approaches. In addition, racism and sexism among pupils can make this a difficult learning model to establish. But where teachers have set out sensitively to use collaborative learning, drawing on the strengths of all the children as one way of overcoming race and gender divisions, considerable learning and social achievements have been noted (Hester, 1982; Wiles, 1981).

5 Children Must be Integrated into Regular School Activities From the Start

Separating bilingual children from their English speaking peers will be totally counterproductive. Special reception units or schools are not effective in helping the children to learn English. Worse, they are socially and culturally divisive. They accentuate feelings of separateness and difference and are a form of institutional racism. It is essential that children feel part of the mainstream school from the very beginning, taking part in its routines and rituals and having access to the full range of activities available for all children. They must not be made to feel like spectators on the sidelines — on the fringes of the real world (Hester, 1982; Ministry of Education, British Columbia, 1979; Hargreaves, 1984).

This is not intended to suggest a levelling process: to simplify everything to the point where the second language learner can understand and then everyone will be able to do it. A more constructive approach is to analyze not the language but the learning task. This is not as easy as it sounds, for there is frequently a mismatch between the tasks children are asked to do and their ability to do them (DES 1978; Bennett and Desforges, 1984). A closer look at the educational demands being made on children and a greater understanding of how children can be supported as they come to terms with new learning — exploring tasks collaboratively, sharing each other's perceptions, clearer visual support — will be of benefit to all the children.

If time has to be spent in special second language classrooms it should be minimized. Research has shown that the more children are taken out of the mainstream class for special help with their English the less progress they are likely to make in the learning of the language. Although surprising at first, this finding is entirely consistent with what we now know about the factors which are conducive to language learning. Some of the problems of a withdrawal system are: it removes children from a natural model of the target language — the native speakers in the class; the adult model becomes the only model available, tiring and difficult to handle naturally; the sessions therefore tend to be adult dominated — the least productive talk situations; organizationally it is difficult, there tend to be children at the same linguistic level and therefore of varying ages from a range of classes, or children of similar ages and varying linguistic levels (in which case, why withdraw?). Although, in theory, smaller numbers should mean more individual attention, in practice it is difficult to make this extra support effective because it is hard to liaise with the various class teachers and provide something which will help the work going on in the mainstream. Furthermore, withdrawal usually has negative connotations (slow learners, remedial reading) and is often resented by the children.

Focusing on language rather than content is unproductive; few people are interested in language for its own sake because language is a tool for communication, not an end in itself. The social arguments against reception units are also relevant to withdrawal models. Schools must consider these very seriously and, if they still believe that some form of withdrawal help is useful, the groups should be linguistically mixed (both monolingual and bilingual children) and the work done in them directly related to the work undertaken by the teacher and children in the mainstream class (Fathman, 1976).

6 The Regular Classroom as the Context for Second Language Learning

The most appropriate language learning situation for a second language student is with a group of pupils of her/his own age in their normal classroom. This statement is the logical outcome of everything that has been said before. For all the reasons listed above, a second language learner will learn most effectively in the mainstream class. Any additional support should be given to bilingual children in the regular class in curriculum-related areas in conjunction with the class/subject teacher (Ministry of Education, British Columbia, 1979; Hargreaves, 1984).

7   Using language to Learn the Language

Many language courses set out to teach learners sentences they will never hear or be called on to use: 'This is a book; That is a window,' 'The boy is posting the letter,' etc. They are sometimes required to answer in 'full' sentences (whatever they are) and corrected for using dialect forms which may go uncorrected in their peers. However, it is right and proper that bilingual children should develop the full range of language use of their peers from the informal codes of the playground to the formal style appropriate for the examination paper (Widdowson, 1980).

That being so, there is no pre-structured course or published text book that is satisfactory for teaching a second language. Most teachers are very disappointed when they learn this. They usually believe that somewhere out there the perfect book for Rezia exists, if only they knew where to find it. If they could sit her down with it for a few months, she'd then be able to join in the classroom learning without more ado. But language can't be learnt by communing with a book or by practising structured drills. It has to be worked at untidily with real people in real situations. And the real learning in any one class is specific to that class; indeed the same is true about the curriculum in relation to the school. There are no short cuts. A second language must be taught within the context of other school subjects.

Children learn their first language not as an end in itself but as a means of learning about and acting in the world around them. The most effective language teaching uses the language to enable children to develop cognitively and socially and is based on the learning requirements of the total school curriculum. It follows, therefore, that everyone on the staff must be involved and have a responsibility for bilingual children — not just the English Department or the second language teaching specialist (Saville-Troike, 1976; Hargreaves, 1984).

Wider Issues

I hope I have now made it clear that when minority children's first language is promoted by the school, bilingualism can be a positive force in their development. Being bilingual should be a positive advantage, intellectually, socially and culturally. That this is so often not the case is due, not to the fact of bilingualism itself, but to the attitudes towards it held by the wider society. Even this needs qualifying. Most people would agree that speaking French or Italian or Russian as well as English is admirable, whereas speaking a South Asian language and English seems less worthy of note — another example of racism. Until recently, many teachers didn't even think it important to find out about their bilingual children's linguistic skills. Furthermore, because society's attitudes were negative about these skills, many children became embarrassed about using their home language.

Happily, the tide seems to be turning and schools which have introduced some community language teaching have noted the positive effect this has on the children's sense of pride and their general attitude to school. Even where it is not possible to offer community language teaching as part of the curriculum, it is possible for teachers to show that they recognize and respect their children's bilingual skills.

It is equally important to recognize that the quality of parent-child communication in the home is crucial for children's full development. Parents should never be exhorted to use the second language at home unless they choose to do so. In the past, it was not uncommon for teachers, speech therapists and home visitors to advise parents of bilingual children to use only English at home. This they did with the best of intentions, thinking it would help the children to develop their English more rapidly. It was misguided, however. For as we now realize, it is the quality of the interaction that is important, not the specific language through which the communication is mediated. Communicative competence in one language is likely to lead to enhanced communication in another. Nothing is gained by suggesting to parents that they attempt to communicate with their children in a language in which they themselves may not be competent. In fact, it is the development of linguistic concepts *per se* that is central to children's overall intellectual and academic development. If these concepts have been developed in the first language, they can easily be transferred to a second language. With young bilinguals it is interesting to note that when they have acquired a new word in one language it tends to occur quite soon afterwards in the second, provided there has been adequate exposure to it (Cummins, 1982; Saunders, 1982).

Contrary to earlier research reports, which tended to treat bilingualism almost as a disease, recent research from many parts of the world indicates that being bilingual can actually have a positive effect on intelligence and can give bilingual children certain cognitive advantages over their monolingual peers. Bilingual children become aware much earlier of the arbitrary nature of language. They learn that things can be referred to in two different ways for example, 'dog'/'Hund'). This probably helps them to become aware of language as an abstract system, an important notion, for example, when learning to read. Other studies have shown that bilingual children have greater cognitive flexibility, greater social sensitivity and greater adeptness at creative thinking (Peal and Lambert, 1962; Cummins, 1982). One thing is certain: we have no reason to be frightened of the effects of bilingualism. On the contrary, it makes sense to see it as a resource to be cherished.

In Conclusion: Some Questions That Need To Be Asked by Heads and Administrators

The topics that have been raised throughout this chapter have many implications for all educationists. In particular, they have implications at the level of school organization — how best to use teachers to support bilingual children. The paper has been largely concerned with classroom organization — how best to create a context in which bilingual children can be given maximum support for their learning and their language development (both first and second). It has also drawn attention to the appropriate ethos that needs to be created — the recognition of other languages and cultures and the creation of a strong anti-racist perspective which enables all children to feel welcome and able to take an active part in the life of the school. Furthermore, the importance of parental and community contact has been emphasized, with the implication that everyone involved with the children should be working in harmony, with the children's needs the central issue.

It seems appropriate, therefore, to conclude with some specific questions that those responsible for educational provision would do well to consider:

1   Is support for bilingual children totally or at least mainly within the mainstream? If not, are staff trying to move towards this — given what we know about how children learn language?
2   If there is specialist support for second language learners, what structures exist for ensuring that this is given within the context of the mainstream curriculum?

3 Is there continuing staff discussion about how learning can be made more accessible to bilingual children within the mainstream class, including the use of mother tongues?
4 To what extent is there provision for collaborative/small group learning — an important organizational issue if bilingual children are to be given maximum support?
5 Is there an agreed 'language across the curriculum' policy and are staff consistent in their response to the English of bilingual children?
6 Do staff agree that all teachers and all departments have a responsibility for the children's language development and not just the language post holder, those in the English Department and the second language specialists?
7 Do staff know if children are going to mother tongue classes after school or at weekends and has there been any discussion of this issue with the parents and teachers of such classes?

Note

An earlier version of this chapter, under the title 'Learning a Second Language', was published in *English Magazine*. ILEA, Summer 1984.

Children's Difficulties in Learning to Compose

Carl Bereiter and Marlene Scardamalia

In the next two chapters we have chosen, quite deliberately, to focus on the production, rather than the reception, of written language. It is here that we see the most significant developments to be occurring. This chapter is concerned with the kind of thinking involved in creating written text. For teachers that means trying to understand what goes on in their pupils' minds while they are composing and that is where cognitive psychology can be helpful. The chapter leaves one in no doubt about the complexity of the 'information processing load' involved in successful composing and, to many teachers, the approach to writing adopted by Bereiter and Scardamalia should prove more useful than the more traditional concern with details of transcription.

From the perspective of this chapter it might be argued that expressive or 'creative' writing, valuable as it is in the early years, and indeed later, as a means of motivating children to write can also become a 'coping strategy' for evading the real purposes (and problems) of skilled writing. The 'knowledge-telling strategy' the authors describe has even more far-reaching implications. As they remind us, we don't really know when or how to intervene in children's writing in order to be most helpful. This chapter shows how that area of professional incomprehension might be reduced.

Defining the Problem

For cognitive psychologists approaching the difficulties of learning to write, there are two attractive hypotheses that seem, in advance of research, to be sufficient to account for childhood's difficulties with written communication. One is information processing load — the overall burden of things to keep in mind when writing. The other is limited development of discourse schemata — mental structures that guide the writer in structuring a composition. As soon as one starts to consider all the things one has to worry about more-or-less simultaneously in writing — from the vagaries of spelling to the possible reactions of an unknown reader — it starts to appear that the work of the writer is somewhere beyond the work of the air traffic controller in its information processing load. The discourse schema hypothesis gains its force from the apparently greater facility children have with narrative in comparison to expository writing (Hidi and Hildyard, in press). The cause that comes immediately to mind is children's greater exposure to the narrative form. (But does anyone seriously believe that if parents read their toddlers bedtime essays instead of bedtime stories the situation would be reversed?)

We were initially much taken with these hypotheses ourselves (Bereiter, 1980). There is substantial truth in both of them, but, as we have come to understand somewhat better the problems children actually contend with in learning to write and how they cope with them, these hypotheses have lost their central position as explanations. Although the options available to writers are limited by the amount of information they can keep in mind, it seems to be mainly the expert, serious writer who strains against such limitations. Those writers ironically labelled 'novices' seem to have found handy ways around the heaviest information processing burdens (Bereiter and Scardamalia, in press; Scardamalia, Bereiter and Goelman, 1982). As for discourse schemata, children early, and by rather mysterious means, shape their compositions according to discourse schema constraints. Their problems seem not to lie at that level, but rather at the level of intentional control over those schemata.

Learning to compose, we have come to believe involves massive upgrading of a discourse production system adapted at all levels to the conditions of dialogue, upgrading it so that it can function autonomously in a goal-oriented manner. In the following sections we summarize the developmental findings on which this belief is based.

Research Findings

The research drawn on in the following discussion consists largely of about seventy experiments conducted since 1976 by ourselves and colleagues in the Toronto Writing Research Group. These experiments have used subjects from age seven to adult, but have tended to focus on the ten to fourteen year age range and on expository writing, especially the writing of opinion essays. It is in this age range that we find students no longer preoccupied with difficulties of the written medium but still in the process of assembling strategies for meeting the demands of prose composition, as they see them. For comparative descriptions of adult competence, both expert and novice, we rely largely on the research of Hayes and Flower (1980).

The difficulties children have in learning to compose appear in five major areas:

1 Sustained Production

Conversation is geared to turn-taking, and there are indications that young writers have some difficulty adapting to the absence of external signals to say more. Prompting students to say more, after they had reportedly written all they could, was found to double their output, while sustaining coherence and improving the rated quality of their essays (Scardamalia, Bereiter and Goelman, 1982). The prompts contained no suggestions as to what to say, and thus appear to have served simply as external triggers of discourse production. Sustaining production depends on many other factors as well, of course, but somehow the young writer must acquire a functional substitute for the nods and 'uh-huh's' of an encouraging listener.

2 Memory Search

Besides nods and 'uh-huh's,' conversation usually provides abundant memory retrieval cues. The absence of these external cues in writing, and the consequent need for deliberate memory search, poses a difficulty that all writers have to contend with except on those occasions when spontaneous recall takes over. For children the problem is endemic. 'I can't think of anything else to write' is a perennial child's complaint, and to avoid it teachers often go to great lengths through pre-writing or motivational devices to ensure that spontaneous retrieval will suffice.

Thinking aloud protocols suggest two processes going on when skilled writers confront an assignment that requires extensive memory search. The first is a preliminary inventory taking, signalled by statements such as, 'Let's see — what do I know about this?' In this process a writer may, for instance, decide to rule out a certain approach to the topic for lack of a sufficient quantity of information.

The other process, documented by Flower and Hayes (1980a), is the progressive elaboration of constraints which serves as memory search criteria — in other words, getting a clearer idea of what one is looking for. In over a hundred thinking-aloud protocols from students 14 years old and younger we detect only occasional hints of these processes.

Taking inventory to see what knowledge they have available is evidently an unfamiliar task for children. As a preliminary to one writing experiment (Scardamalia, Bereiter, and Woodruff, 1980), we interviewed 10 and 12 year olds to ascertain topics about which they considered themselves to know quite a bit or very little. The children consistently found this to be a difficult task and hardly any of them could come up with as many as five topics of either kind.

With external cuing, such as occurs in group brainstorming sessions, children easily produce an abundance of ideas on any reasonable topic. Left to themselves they quickly bog down. Almost any sort of external stimulus is eagerly seized on as a cue to aid memory search. Even critical evaluative statements were reported by most children to make writing easier by helping them think of what to write next (Scardamalia and Bereiter, 1983).

The only procedure we have found to facilitate memory search without external cues is, after assigning a composition topic, to have children list isolated words that they think they might use in the compositions they are about to write (Anderson, Bereiter, and Smart, 1980). This procedure probably has a priming effect, resulting in activation of areas of memory relevant to the composition topic, but it lacks the inventory-taking function, which seems vital to strategic planning.

3   Discourse Structure

There is little reason to doubt that structural knowledge of some kind shapes children's compositions. In the case of narrative, this has been demonstrated even at very young ages (Stein and Trabasso, 1982). In other genres, where structural constraints are weaker, the case is harder to demonstrate (Hidi and Hildyard, in press). There is some experimental evidence — for instance, in the longer time to begin writing when given an unconventional rather than a conventional order of discourse elements (Paris, 1980). More generally, children's productions are almost never completely formless or inappropriate to the intended genre. They must surely be influenced by structural schemata of some sort.

Thinking-aloud protocols of adults show them to make explicit use of concepts such as thesis, proof, introduction, conclusion, character, situation, and example (Flower and Hayes, 1980b; Scardamalia and Paris, 1982). These explicit items of discourse schema knowledge are especially used in organizing a composition or assessing its overall adequacy. Organizational and strategic planning are rarely seen in children's protocols, and evidence of explicit knowledge of discourse elements is also rare.

Children as young as ten appear to have some conscious access to discourse structure knowledge, but there is no correlation between the amount of knowledge they can report and the amount they display in their writing (Bereiter and Scardamalia, 1982). When we stated earlier that we did not consider lack of discourse schema knowledge to be a central factor in children's writing difficulties, it was because of indications that children already have a great deal of schema knowledge. Limitations appear more in uses they can make of it than in its availability.

4   Goal-Directed Planning

When they are told that adults often think for fifteen minutes or more before starting to write on a simple composition topic, elementary school children are frequently incredulous and unable to imagine what the adults find to think about. We produced a videotape in which an adult model, thinking aloud, demonstrated with exaggerated distinctness, several common varieties of planning: reviewing relevant knowledge, setting goals, anticipating difficulties, anticipating reader reactions, and organizing. Ten year olds could not accurately distinguish one kind of planning from another. Twelve and 14 year olds could discriminate, but they showed only a glimmer of ability to carry out the indicated kinds of planning themselves (Burtis, Bereiter, Scardamalia and Tetroe, 1983).

Composition planning does show development during this age period, however. When asked to plan aloud in advance of writing, the younger students essentially generate a first draft orally. The older students generate ideas that are later selected from, added to, and reorganized in producing a text (Burtis *et al.*, 1983). Thus, younger children show little distinction between planning and generating text, whereas by middle adolescence the two have become sufficiently differentiated that it becomes reasonable to speak of the student as being able to create a plan for a text rather than simply rehearsing the text orally in advance of writing it down.

These plans, however, seem to be entirely plans of *what to say*. Only in skilled adult writers have we seen plans having to do with achieving some effect. This is not to say that children do not write or aspire to write compositions that convince, that move, etc. Frequently they do. But evidently this is done without conscious planning or problem-solving. Students as old as eighteen show little ability to evaluate the difficulty of rhetorical problems, even when they generate compositions showing a sensitivity to those problems (Bereiter, Baird and Scardamalia 1981; cf, Flower and Hayes, 1980a). The means by which adequate compositions are produced without goal-directed planning will be considered in the section on 'coping strategies'.

5 Revision

Nowhere is the difference between what children can do with help and without help more dramatic than in revision. Unassisted, children throughout the school years are inclined to limit revision to minor cosmetic changes (Nold, 1981). Yet with sufficient feedback, encouragement, and guidance, children as young as 6 have been reported to carry out extensive and ambitious revisions (Graves, 1979). It has been tempting to attribute this discrepancy to youthful egocentrism — that is, to an inability to take the point of view of the reader and to resulting dependence on external feedback. Available evidence indicates, however, that this is not the locus of the problem. Children have shown themselves to be quite capable at evaluating their compositions and recognizing that revisions are needed, but they have trouble pin-pointing difficulties and taking appropriate remedial actions (Bartlett, 1982; Cattani, Scardamalia and Bereiter, 1982; Scardamalia and Bereiter, 1983).

Children's difficulties with revision are, we believe, simply a reflection of their difficulties with composition as a whole. These difficulties are dramatized because purposeful revision cannot proceed without some mental representation of intended text, against which actual text can be tested. Such representations are also important in original composition, but as we shall see in the next section, there are ways to get along without them. Children's abilities to recognize needs for revision can be attributed to their having global intentions against which general impressions of text can be tested. But in order for effective action to be taken, more specific subgoals are needed. Having the goal of writing an exciting story is not enough. One needs, for instance, the subgoal of building up suspense about a particular impending event. When we ask children about their choices in composition — whether during planning, writing, or revision phases — we seldom hear any references to goals other than global ones. There is the occasional child who, like the expert adult writer, displays a variety of subgoals relevant to specific choices of content and language. Thus, the child may say of a certain exaggerated expression. 'I thought it would grab people.' With most children, however, no amount of probing brings such subgoals to light, which suggests that only global goals are operating.

Lacking the representations of goals and texts that would make it possible for them to mentally test revisions, children find revision a fairly arbitrary process. Seemingly limitless possibilities of change exist, but they cannot tell whether a particular change will fit their global objectives until they try it. The odds are that it will not, which makes revision an unprofitable enterprise.

Coping Strategies

The preceding list of difficulties might make it seem as if writing should be all but impossible for school-age children. The difficulties, we maintain, are real, and place significant limitations on what children can do in written composition. Both children and teachers, however, show an impressive facility in adapting to and finding ways around these limitations — to such a degree that in many classroom writing activities one sees scarcely any evidence of the difficulties that a little experimental probing reveals.

Many writing difficulties can be side-stepped, for instance by letting children write whatever they want. Besides the obvious motivational advantage, this policy eliminates the need for memory search and conscious formulation of purpose, because the discourse consists primarily of material that has come spontaneously to mind. When more task-like writing is assigned, teachers have a variety of ways to compensate for those aspects of writing competence that are not sufficiently developed in children. Pre-writing activities, such as group discussions, serve to activate relevant knowledge and intentions. Social devices such as teacher-pupil conferences and peer response introduce conversational elements into the composing process, with the various kinds of cuing that conversation provides. If serious revision is undertaken at all, it is usually aided by direct suggestions from teacher or peers.

The net result of these adaptations is to make it possible for children to express themselves through written discourse while relying on a discourse production system that has been only minimally modified from its original conversational purpose. Even in the most supportive environment, however, students need to develop some kind of control structure that will enable them to generate extended text. By the age of 12, most of the children we have studied seem to have consolidated a strategy that enables them to produce appropriate text in response to virtually any writing assignment. The strategy enables them to do this, however, by circumventing rather than overcoming most of the difficulties noted in the preceding section.

The strategy is one we call 'knowledge telling.' It can be summarized by the following rule: *Whatever the writing assignment, translate it into a topic. Then tell what you know about the topic, observing genre constraints.* The rule applies to expository writing, including such tasks as essay examinations. We may note in passing that some students show a predilection for translating assignments into story assignments, and do so on unlikely occasions. The knowledge-telling strategy, however, fits with observations on hundreds of student compositions on a variety of expository tasks. Whatever their weaknesses might be, students' compositions are almost invariably appropriate to the topic and the specified or implied genre.

A commonplace application of the knowledge-telling strategy is the following: Given an assignment to compare theory A with theory B, the student tells what he or she knows about theory A and then does the same for theory B, making no systematic comparison of the two theories. Even though instructors recognize that such responses fail to come to grips with the assignment, they will seldom give them a failing grade, provided the responses demonstrate an adequate amount of knowledge about the specified topics.

The knowledge-telling strategy is inferred from a variety of indications:

1   The fact that thinking-aloud protocols of young writers consist almost entirely of content generation, with no evidence of conscious goal-directed planning (Burtis *et al.*, 1983).

2   The tendency of novice writers to present information in the order of its acquisition (Flower, 1979), which suggests unplanned retrieval.

3   The tendency of novice writers to re-examine the assignment for cues when stuck (Flower and Hayes, 1980a) — which we take to be a search for additional topics to use as probes — whereas experts consult their goals.

4   The weak connections among sentences in student texts — especially the lack of connection between widely separated parts — suggesting a forward-acting or additive approach to text generation (McCutchen and Perfetti, 1982).

5   The primacy of content-search problems, as noted previously.

6   The ability of children to compose essays using prescribed sequences of discourse elements (Paris, 1980), an indication of the regulative force of discourse schemata.

7   The finding that when students were provided with lists of structurally relevant sentence openers to choose from ('On the other hand...,' 'Another reason...,' etc.) they unanimously asserted that this made composition easier, although the resulting compositions were essentially indistinguishable from those they normally produced (Bereiter and Scardamalia, 1982) — suggesting that these schema-based prompts fitted in with their existing strategy and served as aids to retrieval.

8   The appearance of an analogous topic-based simplifying strategy in children's reading comprehension (Scardamalia and Bereiter, in press).

9   The scarcity of revision in children's writing (Nold, 1981), which suggests, according to the reasoning advanced earlier, a lack of operations involving goal representations.

Implications For Teaching:

The knowledge-telling strategy is clearly adaptive to school writing demands. It permits at least a minimally adequate response to any assignment for which the student has relevant knowledge; it turns the assignment into an aid to memory search; it apparently also mobilizes discourse schema knowledge in a generative capacity; it virtually eliminates the need for goal-directed planning or problem solving; it eliminates the need for mental manipulation of large text units, allowing composition to proceed on more or less of a sentence-by-sentence basis; and it avoids the burden on working memory that arises from simultaneous attention to a variety of constraints or subgoals. At the same time, the knowledge-telling strategy gives scope to students' creative and expressive impulses, to the extent that these can be realized through serial generation.

Under the guidance of a helpful teacher, who compensates for the missing goal-related dimension, students using the knowledge-telling strategy can often produce impressive pieces of writing. Left to their own devices, knowledge-tellers are unlikely to produce truly effective compositions, but their strategy may still enable them to meet most of the everyday demands of life in a literate society. It seems likely, however, that much of the bad writing we are exposed to in daily life results from persisting use of the knowledge-telling strategy. For instance, military training manuals have been criticized for stating information about the topic instead of teaching the user of the manual to perform (Human Resources Research Organization, 1977). Many of the examples cited in the criticism were not badly written in the sense that they would receive bad marks from an English teacher, but they would nonetheless be frustrating to a user because of their failure to perform their basic instructional function. In order to write an effective training manual, the writer must have a composing strategy that can translate goals which specify what the reader is supposed to do into goals representing intended text. This a knowledge-telling strategy cannot do.

The knowledge-telling strategy can be readily appreciated as a way children manage to cope with a task that is initially too complex for them. It could thus take its place among the many other simplifications that children reveal in their cognitive behavior and subsequently outgrow (*cf.*, Case, 1978; Siegler, 1981). But school practices, in turn, appear to be finely adapted to the knowledge-telling strategy and thus (unwittingly, of course) support its perpetuation.

Although instruction must always adapt to children' limitations, there is danger if it adapts too much. We are concerned, for instance, about the uncritical enthusiasm for pre-writing activities — for discussions, art projects, dramatic productions, field trips, film viewings, self-awareness exercises — anything that serves to prime the literary pump. It is impossible to be opposed to such activities. They have value in their own right, and one does, after all, expect writing to grow out of other experiences and not to exist in a world by itself. But it is important, at the same time, for teachers to realise that by arranging these pre-writing activities they are compensating for young writers' typical lacks. To the extent the goals and content all come out of the pre-writing experience, they do not come out of the writing process itself. And the recurrent claim of mature writers is that writing is more than a way of getting down what they already know and feel. It is a way of developing their knowledge and feelings.

The ideal course — and the one no doubt intuitively followed by talented teachers — is a middle course between leaving students too much on their own and doing too much for them. Research on children's composing processes may make it easier to find that middle course. One important conceptual advance that research on the composing process has helped to bring about is the realization that what goes on in the mind during pre-writing activities or while re-reading a finished draft is all part of the composing process. And so, to take over parts of those activities — by Socratic questioning, by making editorial suggestions, or whatever — is to take over some part of the student's composing process. As Vygotsky emphasized, the role of the adult in promoting learning often consists of taking over part of a complex process and then gradually transferring it to the child, as the child grows in competence. But what parts of the writing process to take over, how best to transfer them to the child, and when — these are questions that require quite penetrating research to answer.

Spontaneous and Scientific Concepts: Young Children's Learning of Punctuation

Courtney B. Cadzen, Patricia Cordeiro and Mary E. Giacobbe

Young children's difficulties with reading have been extensively investigated and, as regards writing, so have their problems with spelling. Spelling research has generally been concerned with conventional spelling but, more recently, there has been widespread interest in invented spellings and what these can tell us about young children's understanding of the writing system. It is surprising, therefore, that there has not been a similar interest in punctuation because, as this chapter shows, their 'errors' repay careful study and can provide information that has clear implications for classroom practice.

'Common sense', a notoriously poor guide for the teaching of writing, is often taken to suggest that punctuation errors, especially mis-placed full stops, lead to 'bad habits' and should be eliminated by teacher instruction and correction. The research reported here, however, shows that assumption to be false. Young children's punctuation errors are shown to be another indication of their active involvement in the learning process, representing hypotheses about English syntax. The research data also show that such errors are gradually replaced by 'closer and closer approximations to the adult system'. Learning to write in sentences is an essential basis for further development in writing. This chapter suggests that teachers who place undue emphasis on 'correct' punctuation do not help children to develop such understanding.

Introduction

More than ten years ago, one of us wrote that, 'One reason why language is such a difficult subject for curriculum planners is that we do not understand the relationship between what is in some way *learned* and what can be *taught*' (Cazden, 1973, pp. 135–6). Emig, quoting that statement in a recent article, goes on to caution against what she calls (after Piaget) 'magical thinking' — the belief that we have, by our actions, caused something that in fact has an independent source (Emig, 1981). In the case of writing, she cautions against the tempting belief that children learn only because, and only what, we as teachers explicitly teach. Our intent here is not to argue about the relative importance of learning *vs.* teaching, or — to use Vygotsky's terms — spontaneous *vs.* scientific concepts, but to ask again about the relationship between the two.

In *Thought and Language* (1962), Vygotsky defined spontaneous concepts as those — like *brother* — that are learned directly from experience, unmediated by definitions or explanation; scientific concepts, by contrast, are those — like *exploitation* — that begin in the verbal definitions and explanations of a more knowledgeable other. What we call 'teaching' is necessary for the latter, but they cannot be absorbed ready-made in parrot-like repetition. Vygotsky reminds us that both spontaneous and scientific concepts evolve with the aid of strenuous mental activity on the part of the child:

> In working its slow way upward, an everyday [or spontaneous] concept clears a path for the scientific concept and its downward development. It creates a series of structures necessary for the evolution of a concept's more primitive, elementary aspects, which give it body and vitality. Scientific concepts in turn supply structures for the upward development of the child's spontaneous concepts toward consciousness and deliberate use. Scientific concepts grow down through spontaneous concepts; spontaneous concepts grow upward through scientific concepts (p. 109).

For concrete material with which to consider this relationship, we will describe a longitudinal study of first grade (6 year old) children's progress in coping with one set of written language conventions — three punctuation marks: possessive apostrophe 's', quotations marks, and periods. We focus on punctuation not at all because we think it should become more important to young writers or their teachers. Punctuation, like spelling and handwriting (or typing), is an aspect of the transcription — not the composition — process. (See Bartlett, 1981 and Smith, 1982 for excellent discussions.) It is the composition of ideas, not their transcriptions on paper, that is the first focus of writers' attention. Nonetheless a longitudinal analysis of children's learning of punctuation, especially of periods, illuminates some details of the relationship between spontaneous and scientific concepts, even here where one might assume that explicit adult instruction in the conventions of written English could be the only source of growth.

We will first describe the classroom in which this learning took place, and then report children's learning by means of both summary statistics and examples of texts. When children's actual spelling is irrelevant to the discussion, our standardized translation is presented in lower case letters. Later, in examples 4–12, we preserve children's spelling in CAPS. We will then refer briefly to related research on children's early learning of both spelling and punctuation, and end with suggested implications for teaching.

The Classroom as a Writing Environment

One of us, Mary Ellen Giacobbe, was the classroom teacher. Her classroom was one of the sites for Donald Graves's research (and is pictured on the cover of his most recent book: Graves, 1983). The children's writings analyzed here come from the year after the Graves research team had left.

They entered an activity-centered classroom where children viewed themselves and their classmates as individuals who had thoughts and ideas worth communicating to others, and who knew writing was a powerful aid in this communication. From the first day of school, these children were writing, not dictating to the teacher but writing themselves (Giacobbe, 1982).

Given a 9 × 12-inch blank journal to draw and write in, they all drew pictures and wrote about them. When the children finished their initial journals (in four to six weeks), they shifted to picture story paper, booklets, etc. There was a writing center with an assortment of writing materials for rehearsing, drafting, revising and editing.

Giacobbe's role as teacher was to 'conference' with the children about their writing. (See Sowers, 1984, for a discussion of conferencing, with many examples.) She held four types of conferences, with content always the first focus and skills the last. About the skills or 'editing' conference she says:

> When the content is as the writer intends it to be, the child is taught one skill in the context of his writing. For instance, if

there is a lot of dialogue in a particular story, I might teach the child how to use quotation marks. If the child uses that skill in the next piece of writing, I ask about the usage, and the child decides if it should be added to the list of skills s/he is responsible for during the editing stage of future writing.

Located in the writing center were two writing folders for each child. The first folder, for work in progress, served as a record-keeping device for both the writer and the teacher. All the titles of books written are listed on the cover. Inside the cover on the left is a list of possible topics to write about (compiled by each child). On the right is the list of skills the writer is responsible for during the editing stage of any piece of writing. On the back of the folder is space for the teacher to keep a record of skills known and skills taught. The other folder was for accumulated work.

Children's Learning

The material for our study of the learning of punctuation comes from these two sets of folders. We had the complete folders of all twenty-two children for the entire first-grade year, and we had information on just when (from September to May) each child was taught (and sometimes re-taught) a particular skill. We realise that, especially in a classroom like this, children have many sources of information in addition to the teacher: notably, other children and a wide variety of written texts, and we have no way retrospectively to track children's use of these sources for information about punctuation. But we can locate the time when an individual child received explicit individual instruction from the teacher.

From the list in each child's folder, we can tell that the three punctuation marks taught to most children were periods (thirteen of the twenty-two children), possessive apostrophes and quotation marks (six children each). The only skill taught to as many children was the spelling of the verb ending -*ing*, and it is worth stopping to look at the pattern of learning here for later contrast with the more difficult punctuation tasks. [See Table 1]

To put Table 1 into words: for the thirteen children who were taught, their texts included 238 verbs requiring –*ing*. Forty-nine of these were spelled correctly, for a percentage correct of 21. There were forty-two verbs in the thirteen stories about which the teaching took place. Then from the time of teaching until the end of the year, these same thirteen children's texts included 706 –*ing* verb forms of

Table 1. *Learning to Spell the Verb Ending — ing*

	Number of Children	Percentage Correct Before Teaching (Number Correct/Number of Opportunities)	Opportunities at Time of Teaching	Percentage Correct After Teaching (Number Correct/Number of Opportunities)
Taught	13	21 (49/238)	42	93 (655/706)
		Percentage Correct Throughout Year (Number Correct/ Number of Opportunities)		
Not Taught	9	82 (293/358)		

which 655 were correctly spelled, for a percentage correct of 93. For the nine children not taught, their spelling of *ing* is summarized once for the entire year: 358 instances of which 293 were correct, for a percentage of 82. (The data for punctuation will be presented in this same form.)

It is clear from these figures that *–ing* gave these children little trouble. The thirteen children who were taught it obtained virtual mastery (usually in the next story). And the nine children who were not taught (presumably because the teacher felt they didn't need it) developed nearly the same mastery, evidently from other sources of information.

The three punctuation marks the teacher decided the children most needed were periods, possessive apostrophes and quotation marks. Coincidentally, these exemplify the two major purposes of punctuation in English: *segmentation* of words into units by periods, commas etc., and *identification* of units such as a possessive ending (and not a plural) by an apostrophe (Quirk and Greenbaum, 1973). Quotation marks share both functions — both separating and identifying direct speech. Because periods pose especially difficult problems, we leave them until last.

Six children were taught to use an apostrophe to mark possession. Typically, the teacher would say, 'When something *belongs* to someone else, we put one of these little marks [showing as she speaks]. We call that an "apostrophe" and we add the *s*. That lets the reader know that *my friend's house* [pointing to the child's text] means the house belongs to your friend; it doesn't mean "lots of friends".' We counted as correct any mark floating above the line, followed by an *s*. The summary story presented in the same form as for *ing* shows both slower learning and a more significant role for instruction. (See Table 2)

Note that these charts show only opportunities and the number of them filled correctly; that is, only errors of omission are tabulated here. Errors of commission, placing those marks where they *don't* belong, will be discussed separately.

Six children were taught to use quotation marks. Typically the teacher would say, 'Someone is talking on this page. If we could hear her talking, what would she say? [Child reads] Well, we have some marks that we put around the words people say, before the first word and after the last.' We counted as correct any floating marks of any shape. Table 3 presents the summary story. It is very similar to the possessive apostrophe in both rate of progress and the benefits of instruction.

Table 2. *Learning to Use Possessive Apostrophes*

	Number of Children	Percentage Correct Before Teaching (Number Correct/Number of Opportunities)	Opportunities at Time of Teaching	Percentage Correct After Teaching (Number Correct/Number of Opportunities)
Taught	6	16 (3/19)	10	56 (31/55)
		Percentage Correct Throughout Year (Number Correct/Number of Opportunities)		
Not Taught	16	12 (29/243)		

Table 3. *Learning to Use Quotation Marks*

	Number of Children	Percentage Correct Before Teaching (Number Correct/Number of Opportunities)	Opportunities at Time of Teaching	Percentage Correct After Teaching (Number Correct/Number of Opportunities)
Taught	6	00 (0/28)	12	53 (73/138)
		Percentage Correct Throughout Year (Number Correct/Number of Opportunities)		
Not Taught	16	17 (14/81)		

Periods were taught to thirteen children, and they were retaught more often than the other three conventions combined. Typically, the teacher read aloud a child's story without pauses; when the author objected, she said, 'You read it the way you want it to sound. When you come to a stop, that's probably where we need to put a period.'

We counted as a period any dot between words, grounded or floating. To divide the children's text into sentences for analysis, we were guided by the teacher's transcriptions made during her conferences, and she in turn was guided by the child's oral rendition of the text. So, for example:

(1) 'My dad docked the boat and me and my friends in the boat.'

was punctuated as one sentence in the teacher's transcription and so accepted as correct in our analysis. On the other hand:

(2) 'We went downtown. and to the store.'

was counted as one opportunity for a period (after *store*), one correct (and one incorrect) use. Note that the number of opportunities for correct use of periods is thus also the number of sentences in the total set of compositions according to the teacher's judgment. Children did get credit for deviations from a strict criterion of sentencehood when their use would be considered a legitimate stylistic decision in adult writing. For example, one child wrote a story more than 200 sentences long about his family's 'Cousin convention' in which it was clear that he hated sausage. When he then wrote:

(3) 'We are having pancakes for breakfast. With out sausage.

these periods were both considered correct (even felicitous) use.

Table 4 presents the summary picture for periods. As with possessive apostrophes and quotation marks, the taught children supply needed periods a little more than half the time. In contrast to apostrophes and quotation marks, the untaught children do relatively better from other knowledge sources — whether published texts or their own intuition about structural units we cannot say. We return to the latter possibility below.

Now we want to consider the errors of commission — the punctuation marks that were supplied, but in the wrong place. First, a one-chart summary for all three punctuation marks, and then we'll look at some actual texts to see what the numbers represent.

Table 4. Learning to Use Periods

	Number of Children	Percentage Correct Before Teaching (Number Correct/Number of Opportunities)	Opportunities at Time of Teaching	Percentage Correct After Teaching (Number Correct/Number of Opportunities)
Taught	13	25 (267/1056)	154	57 (1692/2966)
Not Taught	9	Percentage Correct Throughout Year (Number Correct/Number of Opportunities) 49 (817/1821)		

Table 5. Misplaced Punctuation Marks

	Number	Percentage of total correct and mistaken
Quotation marks	4	4 (4/87 + 4)
Possessive apostrophes	38	38 (38/63 + 38)
Periods	475	17 (475/2776 + 475)

With quotation marks, there is little confusion: only four instances where there was no quoted speech, a very small number relative to the total number used (correctly and incorrectly).

With possessive apostrophes, the number of errors is much greater, both absolutely and proportionally. These errors are largely what we call overgeneralizations towards formal similarities of sounds that have different meanings: to plurals like *parade's* and *thing's* and to verbs like *like's* and *live's*. Any system of transcribing speech into writing is necessarily based on a mixture of form and meaning principles. The teacher taught the possessive apostrophe on the strong meaning basis of 'belonging'. But the children — with their attention focused on sounds in their invented spelling — sometimes acted on the basis of sounds here too.

With periods, the possibilities for error are more complex. Consider possible answers to the question the children face: when should words be separated not just by a space but also by a period? Six patterns appear, each representing a hypothesis about the answer to that question: syllabic (relatively rare), interword, endline, end-page, phrase structure and correct. Cognitively, the most interesting alternative, even though no more correct by our conventional standards than the others, occurred between groups of words we call phrases or clauses, structural units intermediate between words on the one hand and full sentences on the other. We refer to this intermediate constituent level as 'phrase structure' placement.

The six patterns can be seen in the following examples:

(4) DN.USOS   dinosaur
     RAS.ING   racing   syllabic
     BL.DID   builded

(5) I.AM.WOKEING.MY.BAEK.AP.THE.HEL.   interword
     I am walking my bike up the hill.

(6) WE PRT ON THE.   endline
     FORTH FOR.
     We parked on the fourth floor.

(7) WAN THE BOWNE WOBPAK IS GON THE CHKDE. endpage
     When the downy woodpecker is gone, the
     chickadee [end of page; the story continues].

(8) ON THE WA HOME. MI CAR IT SPLODID phrase structure
     On the way home my car it exploded.

(9) WON DAY WAN I WAS OWT SID PLAING. 1 end line,
     KERRY CAM OVR. TO PLAY WATHE ME. 1 phrase structure
                                        [after OVR]
                                        1 correct

(10) WE ARE PACING.TO. 1 phrase structure
     GO TO LON MOWTIN. [after PACING]
     We are packing to go to Loon Mountain 1 endline, 1 correct

(11) WE ARE SILE [still] DRIVING TO NEW YOK. 1 phrase structure
     WE TOK MY GRAMS CAR. MY DAD MY MOM AND [after list of names],
     MY BROTHER MY GRAMY AND MY GRAPY. WAT 3 correct
     TO NOW YOK WATH ME.

(12) PETER PAN LIFFS WITH THE LIST BOS. AND 1 phrase strucure,
     WENDY. 1 correct

All the children tried out more than one of these hypotheses, often more than one in a single story (as in examples 9–12). We have given several examples of phrase structure placement (8–12 above) because of what we believe to be its importance as evidence of implicit awareness of constituent structures above the level of the word. By 'awareness' we mean more than is evidenced simply by spontaneous speech production; by 'implicit' we mean that it has not been taught and could not be verbalized with labels for adult categories.

Once we started looking for it, we found additional evidence for such intuitive understanding. We present that evidence in samples from two children's writings: Roy — a child who was taught periods — and who tries out all hypotheses at one time or another; Daren — a child who was *not* taught. When Giacobbe was asked if she could remember why, she said: 'He had a very difficult time expressing himself in speaking and his writing was all over the page, so punctuation conventions just seemed much less important.'

First, there was evidence in the journals in which both children drew pictures and wrote about them in their very first days of school. The overwhelming number of journal entries can be categorized in three constructions, all of which appear in Roy's journal:

1   Noun phrases like:
    (13)   'me and my railroad car'
2   A full sentence consisting of *this is* plus noun phrase as in:
    (14)   'this is my house'
3   A full sentence consisting of agent plus action or activity as in:
    (15)   'I am working in school'

Seventeen of the twenty-two children's journals contained a mixture of constructions like Roy's. One contained only noun phrases, and four contained only full sentences. In the entire set of twenty-two journals there are only two ungrammatical sequences of words.

Daren (the child with difficulties in oral expression) was one of the three children whose journal contained only full sentences, some combined with a continuous story written over more than one day, as in the following:

(16)   'I was in my uncle's airplane before
       the cars were like toys
       The plane landed at last'

His journal also contained one of the two ungrammatical entries we noted:

(17)   'My house. I live'

Second, is the evidence of what we are calling phrase structure placement of periods in the post-journal stories and books. We have not figured out a way to quantify the proportion of these, but we are persuaded that they are not simply random inter-word errors. In addition to examples (8) — (12) above. (18) and (19) show the context of the child's entire page.

Example (18) gives one page from Roy's long multi-page story about fishing. In this case the phrase structure placement of a period occurs at the end of a complete sentence but before the *because* clause:

(18)   if you are fish
       ing under a bridge
       all you are going to
       catch is a sun
       fish. because
       you are in shallow
       water.

Example (19) includes several pages from Daren's multi-page story about space shuttle problems, written over several days as the action unfolded. Here the phrase structure placement occurs after the pilots' names and after 'on Tuesday'.

> (19) I hope they fix the computer.
> The shuttle took off Sunday
> morning John Young and
> Bob Crippin. They were the
> pilots.
> It went around the earth.
> We saw the shuttle land
> on Tuesday. On TV in
> Mrs. Claveon's room
> It was a good landing
> It landed in Houston, California.

Third, there was evidence in some children's division of a text into lines — with or without periods. Here is a particularly clear example from Roy, in which each line — *without exception* — ends at the end of a phrase or clause. Example 20 gives both the original and a more readable translation:

(20)

> The cat climbed up the tree
> because my dog scared the cat
> My mom climbed up the tree
> on the ladder to get the cat
> The cat climbed
> down the tree
> A little of its skin came off.

The important point is that not all groups of words dismissable as 'sentence fragments' have the same structural status, and evidently children intuitively know some important distinctions. They have somehow learned more than we might have thought possible about what Frank Smith (1982) calls 'the structure of meaning' that punctuation indexes, and more than we could have explained even if we had tried. We suggest that the groupings of words we call phrases or clauses are somehow represented in children's internal language structure as spontaneous concepts in Vygotsky's sense, but that externalized evidence of that structural knowledge is apt to get overlooked in our attention to 'shaping' children's behavior to our own standards of correctness.

Related Research

Our work builds on three previous strands of research. First, there is the extensive and well-replicated research on invented spelling begun by Read (1971) and summarized by Clay (1983). Examples (4) — (12) above contain many invented spellings, for example, BLDID, BAEK, CHKDE, WA, MI, etc. Some important generalizations from this research seem to apply to invented punctuation as well.

Children's errors (in terms of the conventional adult system) provide vivid externalizations of spontaneous concepts. In the case of invented spelling, the concepts are about English phonology; in the case of invented punctuation, they are about English syntax. These errors do not become 'bad habits' as behaviorist psychologists would have us believe. Instead, they are gradually replaced by closer and closer approximations to the adult system. At what point in this progression the children can benefit most from explicit teaching of the adult system is an important instructional question. (We do not suggest that the relationship between spontaneous and scientific concepts is the same across domains of knowledge. Hawkins (1978), for example, finds more discontinuity, and even interference, in the transition from everyday concepts to scientific concepts within science itself.)

Second, imaginative experiments on oral language also find evidence of children's phrase structure knowledge. Read and Schreiber (1982) show that seven and eight year old children can easily learn to repeat only the subject noun phrase of a sentence — '*My best friend and I* are selling lemonade.' — but could not learn to repeat a non-constitutive sequence of the same length. From this evidence, Read and Schreiber argue that 'major surface constituents are, in various senses, psychologically real and accessible' (1982, p. 84).

Third, there is a small set of studies on punctuation itself. Bissex (1980) mentions her son's early use of periods between syllables and between words. Edelsky (1983) provides many examples of phrase structure segmentation and punctuation in her rare study of the writing — in Spanish and English — of Hispanic farm worker children in first, second, and third grade bilingual classroom environments that were similar in some ways to Giacobbe's. It was her work that first alerted us to the presence of phrase structure usage. Weaver's (1982) analysis of compositions from grades one to six gives further evidence that punctuation errors are neither random nor mindless. She found that 'sentence fragments' that are punctuated erroneously by our conventional standards change qualitatively with age. Merely counting errors thus masks significant growth. Furthermore, if anyone thinks that children wouldn't make these errors if teachers just gave more drill and practise on proper use, Calkins (1980, as part of the Graves' project) compared the knowledge of punctuation in classrooms like Giacobbe's and those where more traditional instruction was given. She found that third graders who were only taught punctuation during conferences about their own compositions:

> 'could define/explain an average of 8.66 kinds of punctuation. [But] The children who had studied punctuation through classwork, drills and tests, but had rarely written, were only able to define/explain 3.85 kinds of punctuation' (p. 569).

Cronnell (1980) includes a review of other research on punctuation instruction.

Implications for Teaching

In her skills conferences, Giacobbe gave her children explanations of punctuation marks that were based on *meaning* and *function:* the meaning of belonging and of what someone says; and the function of where you want your reader to stop. Such explanations make excellent sense from everything we know about child language acquisition.

Slobin, generalizing from research on the acquisition of some forty different languages, concludes that:

> rules based on consistent meaning — like the regular past tense in English, or the Turkish direct object inflection — are more easily acquired than rules which do not exhibit a one-to-one mapping of meaning onto surface form. (p. 107)

A criterion of consistent meaning fits '*–ing*' and quotation marks perfectly, and possessive apostrophes too (if we forget for the moment their use to identify contractions). But unfortunately, it won't work for periods, which may seem to be the most important punctuation of all.

For periods, no criterion of meaning or function intelligible to a first grade writer is a valid guide to the adult system. A 'sentence' is in the end a formal syntactic category, and explanations that rely on non-syntactic criteria inevitably produce errors. The semantic criterion of a 'complete thought' is meaningless. The speech production criterion of 'where you stop' or 'where your voice falls' — which this teacher used — may well be the most useful approximation for young writers. But one's voice stops, or drops, at the end of many groups of words that are significant phrasal or clausal constituents but are not sentences. And particular rules (not taught in this classroom but often invoked) like 'You can't start a sentence with *because*' are just plain wrong. In speaking we start *utterances* with 'because' all the time (in answer to *why* questions), and even in the most formal terms, sentences can start with 'because' if the 'because' clause is followed by an independent clause (for example, if the first two lines of (20) had been reversed).

The formal difficulties inherent in the correct scientific concept of period should certainly make us reconsider why we usually try to teach them so early. (See Kress, 1982 for an important discussion of 'The development of the concept of "sentence" in children's writing.') And whenever we do try to teach them, one new teaching possibility is suggested by the evidence of intuitive knowledge of constituent structure in the children's phrase structure errors, and in some of the children's division of text into pages (in the journals) and lines later. Where such evidence exists, maybe it would be helpful to go back to it with the child and explain where to put periods ostensively, by pointing: 'Here [lines 2, 4 and 7] but not here [lines 1, 3, 5 and 6]' in (20).

It is possible that until children are old enough to understand terms like 'phrase' and 'clause', both 'independent' and 'dependent', appeal to intuitive structural knowledge provides a firmer basis for growth in understanding than externally imposed definitions that do not take this knowledge into account. As Smith (1982) says:

> How then does a child ever learn to recognize a question, a clause, a sentence ...? The answer is in the same way that children come to recognize dogs, cats, chairs, tables, and just about everything else in the world. Adults do not often try to define for children what constitutes a cat, dog, chair, or table. They do not attempt to teach rules of catness, dogness or whatever. They simply point out instances of each category and leave the children to work out the rules themselves, implicitly. (p. 190)

As regards children's learning of punctuation teachers should realize that progress — while real — is not steady. Especially with periods, alternative hypotheses co-exist, and seemingly correct usage in one composition is followed by errors of both omission and commission in the next. The important message is not to despair, and not to blame either oneself or the child. We must remember that writing is truly a complex activity, and that attention at one level can divert attention from another level, and make previously demonstrated knowledge temporarily disappear from performance (Scardamalia *et al.*, 1982) Moreover, while errors have been our focus in this analysis, the most compelling observation is of how much in these compositions was right. Often, in the face of seemingly monumental concerns, even these beginning writers remembered not only the big ideas but the little details.

Note

Previous versions of this paper were presented by Cazden as an invited address to the Conference on English Education at the annual Convention of the National Conference of Teachers of English, Washington, D.C., November 20, 1983; and appeared in *Language Arts,* 1983, from whom permission to reprint is gratefully acknowledged.

Language Assessment and Language Teaching: Innovation and Interaction

Tom Gorman

Our last two papers are concerned with development in language; with procedures for assessment and what, in fact, constitutes 'linguistic maturity'. This chapter describes how the monitoring of spoken language in Britain is envisaged by the Assessment of Performance Unit. It should be reassuring to those who have reservations about the purposes of the Unit and very helpful to teachers who are themselves faced with the task of assessing development in their pupils' talk. Chapter 4 has already shown that this author does not overstate his case when he claims that there are serious problems to be overcome in 'differentiating and describing types of discourse'.

The view of assessment this paper presents is one that is calculated to help both teachers and pupils. Methods of assessment must be made relevant to the purposes of day-to-day instruction and, the author warns, teachers must be given the time to devise such instruments. That will cost money, of course, but if greater efficiency is the aim it will be money that is well spent. The purpose of monitoring and assessment is to improve performance by both pupils and teachers and 'unless pupils become aware, in specific terms, of ways in which their performance compares to that of their peers, no amount of exhortation or advice from their teachers is likely to radically affect what they do'.

Understanding Assessment

Relatively few teachers consider language assessment to be integral to language teaching. This is understandable given the inadequacy of the assessment procedures generally used to provide evidence about pupils' mastery of language. A recent study of assessment practices in schools in a local authority area in the North of England, for example, reflected what the authors term 'a rather dreary uniformity in assessment practice' (Engel-Clough and Davies, 1984).

In general the matching of appropriate methods of assessment to purposes or intentions is haphazard. Much time-consuming assessment goes on ritualistically with little consideration given as to why it is being carried out, particularly in the marking of written work; the great majority of assessments of pupil performance in all subject areas are based entirely on the evidence of written work. In relatively few schools are the results of assessment used for effective feedback to pupils, for the improvement of teaching or for revision of curricula and few departments give guidance on how marks could be interpreted for the benefit of pupils. Very few schools involve pupils in self-assessment or course assessment. On a more technical level, it is very unusual for methods of scaling for standardizing marks or grades to be adopted within departments or across a school as a whole. Yet that is essential if effective comparison is to be made between a pupil's assessment results in different subjects or in the same subject at different times.

To those who see language assessment as something peripheral to language teaching, the situation I have outlined will cause no disquiet. However, to those who agree with the authors of the Schools Council working paper on the *Practical Curriculum* that 'a teacher's professional expertise consists in a large part of the ability to assess and judge capability', it will give rise to concern (Schools Council, (1981). Such concern has been expressed by members of HM Inspectorate in a number of their reports on schooling. For example, in commenting on the approaches to writing assessment adopted by teachers, the authors of the Inspectorate report on *Aspects of Secondary Education in England* (DES, 1981) noted that '. . . there was wide divergence in the ways in which writing was assessed,' and that in such assessment it was 'difficult for an outsider (and presumably a pupil), to discover any common policy or purpose.' The HMI report on the survey of *Primary Education in England* (DES, 1978) also noted that only in a minority of classes is children's written work regularly used to monitor their progress or used as a basis for teaching. With reference to the teaching of spoken language the 1981 survey of *Primary Education in Northern Ireland* noted that: 'oral work suffers from lack of confidence which many teachers feel . . . when dealing with it because of the difficulty of monitoring progress.' (DENI, 1981).

The disquiet expressed by members of the Inspectorate perhaps arises from the fact that they tend to envisage a broader application for language assessment than do many of the teachers whose work they review. The concern of the authors of the report on Secondary Education in England, referred to above, was stated as follows: 'How far are pupils being equipped to develop their use of language — as learners, as young adults and users of leisure and as individuals in society; in other words, how far have they the language they need to make sense of themselves, of their relationships with other people and of the complexities of the modern world with which they will need to become involved?' (DES, 1981).

A model of language assessment that might begin to approximate to such general requirements would be far more complex than any that has been developed to date. In the real world, pupils use and interpret language for different purposes as a series of discourses in which each utterance occurs in a linguistic and a social context which has to be taken account of, if a reader or listener is to understand a writer's or speaker's communicative intent or purposes. These contexts are manifold and many cannot easily be replicated in the classroom, but far more could be done by teachers to develop methods of assessment that reflect the multifarious demands made on pupils. Teachers of English have had little guidance from professional test-developers to this end. Most of the standardized tests currently available for language assessment embody a model of language in which pupils are required to 'comprehend' discrete words, sentences or brief unrelated extracts, which, because they are uncontexualized, pose problems of interpretation different from and additional to those that are encountered in interpreting authentic discourse.

Up to this point I have made a series of observations, more or less lugubrious, about current practices in language assessment. There are, however, a number of more encouraging developments that should be noted. One is the growing willingness of some Examination Boards and of teachers associated with them to review critically the procedures used in language assessment. The work of John Dixon and Leslie Stratta in their reviews of writing assignments at 16+ provides a case in point (Dixon and Stratta, undated). Secondly, there have been a number of innovations developed by teachers in relation to Mode III CSE Examinations, particularly as regards the use of course-work assessment. These have helped to mitigate the relative lack of differentiation that could formerly be observed in the selection of types and applications of writing undertaken. Another development that is potentially of value is reflected in the increased awareness of the inadequacy of schemes of language assessment that exclude spoken interaction.

Possibly the most significant development, however, has been the stimulus given by the Assessment of Performance Unit (APU) on behalf of the Department of Education and Science, and sister Departments in Wales and Northern Ireland. Their work has led to the development of procedures for monitoring language performance on a national basis and thus served to extend the range of procedures to which teachers can have access. A series of reports on this national monitoring programme has been published by Her Majesty's Stationery Office.

Since it is not possible in this context to elaborate on each of the developments mentioned I will restrict my comments to one particular aspect of that work. My concern will be with the language monitoring programme sponsored by the APU to develop procedures to assess a wide range of activities involving the interpretation or use of sustained talk. I have done this because developments might in due course serve to extend the scope of the procedures currently used in schools to assess language.

There appear to be three main reasons why talk is neither taught nor assessed systematically in the English curriculum. The first relates to the problem of defining the subject area to be taught — of differentiating and describing types of discourse for purposes of instruction or assessment. Secondly, there are the problems of defining the criteria to use in assessment. Thirdly, there are certain methodological problems that need to be overcome. These have to do with methods of tape-recording talk for subsequent assessment, particularly in the context of group discussion or class activity. I would like to discuss the first two of these issues as they seem to be the most significant.

Selecting Tasks for Assessment

In selecting and developing the assessment tasks used in national surveys the following questions were asked: for what purposes do pupils tend to use sustained talk in the classrooms and outside it and who do they address such talk to; and for what purposes and in what contexts do they listen to and interpret such talk? From among the numerous possibilities that suggested themselves the following tasks were selected for inclusion in the national surveys carried out in 1982 and 1983.

*Table 1.   The Interpretation and Production of Sustained Talk
Examples of Task Used (1982/1983 Surveys)*

General Purpose	Specific Task
Describing and Specifying	* Description of an observed object to allow for identification. * Description of a place and explanation of interest. * Description of a sequence of pictures.
Informing/ Expounding	* Interpretation of an account of a process (with diagrams). Exposition of the gist of the account of others. * Interpretation of an account of an experiment. Exposition of the process to others.
Instructing/ Directing	* Practical interpretation of rules of a game. Instructing pupil to play the game. * Constructing a model following a sequence of instructions. * Instructing others how to carry out an experiment.
Reporting	* Report of something learned and explanation of interest. * Report on a favourite book and explanation of interest. * Report of the results of an experiment.
Narrating	* Interpretation of a story, retelling to others. * Interpretation of anecdote narrating personal experience. * Telling a story based on a sequence of pictures.
Arguing/ Persuading	* Explanation of choice of career — argument/justification of point of view. * Interpretation of opposing arguments, restatement of gist of argument and explanation of viewpoint.
Structured Discussion/ Collaboration	* Interpretation and discussion of evidence to decide on proposed action. * Interpretation and discussion of arguments to reach a consensus. * Interpretation and discussion of evidence to reach agreement.
Speculating/ Advancing Hypothesis	* Speculating on the reasons for an experimental finding. * Speculating on the characteristics of a hidden object and production of a diagram.

There are several points to note about these activities.

1   The majority of tasks involve both the *interpretation and production* of sustained talk. Listening and speaking are

not artificially dissociated, though the components are separately assessed.

2   A number of the tasks entail a *sequence of language activities* including reading or writing as a prelude or consequence of talk. The reflect therefore a normal communicative sequence. Again each component in the sequence would normally be separately assessed.

3   They are undertaken by *pairs of pupils or groups made up of pairs*. The first member of each pair is randomly selected from children in the appropriate age-group in a school. Each of these pupils then selects a friend to participate with him or her.

4   Except for a small number of activities intended to show children's performance in communicating with an adult, the teacher/assessor's role is to *establish a context for talk* and *to record* it: not to direct or control it.

5   Primarily because it is difficult to engage in communication while at the same time assessing such communication analytically, a limited range of assessments are conducted on-the-spot, but the taped record allows for *multi-stage assessment*.

The Methods of Assessment

This is done in three distinct stages as follows:

1   Experienced teachers are trained at the NFER to administer and record the pupil's performance and to make initial assessments. At this stage the performance of each pupil is impression-marked in relation to a seven-point scale and in regard to one or more components of each task. Assessors also record a rating for particular tasks which relates to the verbal and non-verbal procedures used by the pupil to hold the attention of the listeners (Orientation to Listener). With respect to certain tasks, such as those that entail giving or interpreting instructions, assessors also take note of the extent to which specific instructions have been accurately conveyed or questions answered, using a check-list for this purpose.

2   The taped records for each pupil are then assembled and impression-marked by a different panel of teachers.

3   A randomly selected sample of the records is then marked

analytically by a third panel of teachers with reference to a range of general and task-specific criteria. For example, *in assessing accounts of a process*, ratings are given in relation to the following criteria:

(a) the identification or selection of the major episodes in the process. (Propositional content).

(b) the adoption of an appropriate rhetorical procedure for listing or referring to the sequence of episodes. (Sequential structure).

(c) choice of syntax and vocabulary. (Lexico-grammatical features).

(d) features including tempo and pacing, hesitation and self-correction, and features associated with verbal assertiveness. (Performance features).

The criteria relating to category (a) are task-specific; others are criteria that apply across tasks.

Procedures in the stages of assessment referred to are summarized in the following chart:

Table 2. Assessment of Speaking

On-The-Spot Assessment: Stage 1	Holistic Scoring: Stage 2	Analytic Scoring: Stage 3
This involves a rating for:	This involves:	This involves:
(i) Overall impression (Scale 1 – 7)	(i) Initial impression marking of *all* taped records (scale 1 – 7)	(i) Focused assessment (Scale 1 – 5) of random sub-samples of taped records
(ii) Orientation to listener (Scale 1 – 5)	(ii) Panels of 12/20 teachers	(a) Propositional/ semantic content (task related criteria)
(iii) Task-specific features (check-list)	(iii) Double marking of taped records.	(b) Sequential structure
		(c) Lexico-grammatical features (Syntax, Lexis).
		(d) Performance features (self-correction, hesitation, tempo etc.)
		(ii) Panels of 8/10 teachers
		(iii) Double marking of taped records.

The evidence obtained from the three types of assessment provides a basis for reporting on the performance of pupils in *different* ways. On-the-spot assessment provides evidence of aspects of performance that are not accessible on the basis of the taped record. For example, pupils frequently supplement their account of a process or an experiment by gesturing or pointing, and substantial information can be conveyed in that way.

The scores derived from the second stage of assessment with reference to the taped records are used as the basis for generalizations about the performance of *groups* of pupils in relation to particular background variables. For example, it is possible on the basis of the double-impression marks to compare the performance of boys and girls in the different regions of England, Wales and Northern Ireland with reference to these scores.

The results of the analytic marking on the other hand are mainly employed to provide a basis for commenting on the specific difficulties encountered and achievements by individual pupils when carrying out the different tasks. For example, pupils generally find it more difficult to describe a picture or to sustain an argument than to give an account of a past experience. Analytic marking makes it possible to investigate such differences in performance in relation to individual performances.

Concluding Comments

One of the conclusions that I would hope might be drawn from the evidence I have given is that language assessment is largely fruitless unless it is able to provide evidence relating to the specific purposes for which the testing is undertaken. In my view, the evidence yielded by the majority of standardized tests of pupils' levels of language attainment, whether or not these tests purport to be 'diagnostic' in function, is irrelevant to the purposes of day-to-day instruction.

If the present situation is to be substantially changed in the future, there would need to be some changes in the normal pattern of professional training given to teachers of English. Most tasks involving the sustained use or interpretation of language impose complex demands on the cognitive, linguistic and social skills that pupils have. In ideal circumstances, teachers would have the training (and the time) to devise task-specific criteria for assessing work produced by their pupils in relation to a general framework of analysis. There are no ready-made schema that can be applied for this purpose, but for native speakers of English, the task of developing such criteria is a less daunting one than is generally realised. There are however certain pre-requisites to such assessment. Firstly, teachers need to become aware of the range of performance that is characteristic of pupils in a particular age group. That is, they need to have sufficient exposure to performances at different levels to make comparative judgments, if required, about the relative performance of individual pupils on specific tasks. In school, teachers need to have the time and opportunity to devise tasks to elicit talk and, where appropriate, to record it and, if necessary, to transcribe it. They also need time to analyze what is recorded and to discuss their analysis with the pupils concerned.

Given the constraints under which most teachers have to work it will be argued, legitimately, that it is Utopian to advocate such a development. In response, I can only state my conviction that there is no substitute for the close analysis of language produced by children in talk and writing. Such analysis is likely to yield more evidence of a kind that can be directly utilized in teaching than any number of more superficial assessments which do not serve to make clear to pupils the ways in which what they say (or write) compares to talking or writing produced by other members of their age-group. Unless pupils do become aware, in specific terms, of ways in which their performance compares to that of their peers, no amount of exhortation or advice from their teachers is likely to radically affect what they do. Such assessment can be and, in my view, should be, an integral part of language teaching.

Socio-Linguistic Development and the Mature Language User: Different Voices for Different Occasions

Gunther Kress

This chapter is placed last because it foregrounds a number of assumptions that are implicit in preceding ones. Chapter 3, on 'Play and Paradoxes', made it clear that what children learn when they are learning language is not socially determined, but educational provision certainly is. Schools are agencies in a socialization process whereby, in democratic societies, the society as well as the individual is seen as open to change. This chapter shows how the language used in institutions and in specialized areas of knowledge creates its own constraints on meaning. Those who have greater power have greater control over the meanings that are created. Kress uses an example from medical discourse to support his argument that the process of categorizing can also depersonalize. In this case the categorizing is for the perfectly responsible purpose of prescribing treatment for people who may come to be seen — and to see themselves — as a particular kind of patient.

The same process can occur in schools and other educational institutions where pupils and students are relatively powerless with respect to the forms of knowledge that are valued. Those who have power must seek to ensure that they do not, albeit unintentionally, exploit it. These institutions are intended to teach socially valued knowledge, but they are also concerned to promote critical thinking about that knowledge. Furthermore, in order to meet other social expectations concerning equality of educational opportunity, the knowledge must be accessible to all. That is why the language curriculum is so important; its purpose, as Kress puts it, is: 'to give students and teachers alike an insight into the full range of abilities and practices implied by the term **linguistic maturity**'.

Linguistic Theory and Educational Practice

Language is a social phenomenon so it follows that linguistic development and maturity cannot be considered in isolation from development and maturity in a much broader sense, as an aspect of social and cultural maturity. Twenty-five years ago (and indeed much more recently than that) such a view was untenable within the mainstream of linguistic thinking. Then, the question of linguistic maturity was conceived of in terms of a quite autonomous language system, dependent if anything on the structure of the mind and derived from general features, considered innate and universal, and seen in purely formal and structural terms.

The shift to a much more widely accepted view of language as a predominantly social and cultural phenomenon constitutes the major change in thinking about language since the late fifties and early sixties. Consequently, although I use the term *sociolinguistic* in the title of this paper, in what follows I hope to make it clear that the distinction between *linguistic* and *sociolinguistic* is a theoretical distortion aimed at maintaining a distinction between that which is held to be autonomously and therefore properly linguistic, and that marginal area where language and society interact. I believe that this is a false dichotomy which cannot and should not be maintained.

Obviously, in making the above claim, I am dealing in generalizations. There have always been socially oriented views of language and some of them have been highly important — even during the last two or three decades. That is certainly true of the work of Malinowski, Firth and Pike, as well as that of Bernstein and Halliday more recently. I am simply attempting to characterize those views which have held dominance, not to indicate the whole range of work in the field. This change of perspective is so far reaching and radical in its effects and implications as to constitute a fundamental re-ordering of the field of language study; it also necessitaties a total rethinking in areas such as the interrelation of linguistic theorizing and educational practice.

The earlier view, with its focus on specific linguistic structures within an autonomously conceived language system led, in educational practice to attempts to measure such things as linguistic abilities, development, deficiencies, maturity, etc., in terms of the command of and facility with specific syntactic forms. Evidence was sought in clause-structures, sentence forms, tenses, embeddings, and in ability to operate certain syntactic transformations (Chomsky, 1969; Menyuk, 1969; Hunt, 1970). The literature in this area is vast — I cite these three influential examples merely to indicate the kind of work I have in mind.

A view of language as a thoroughly social phenomenon must of necessity move from narrow concerns with syntactic structure, and its consequent focus on the sentence (and below-sentence structures) to a concern with socially significant linguistic units and to questions about their interrelation with, provenance in and utter imbrication in social structures. Crucially, the socially relevant unit of language is not the sentence but the text — a term which refers equally to spoken or written language as it occurs in use. Some of the most important work on text is that of Teun Van Dijk (Van Dijk, 1977 and 1979). The work of Michael Halliday and Ruqaiya Hasan on cohesion has also been enormously significant and effective (Halliday and Hasan, 1976) as has Halliday's work on register (Halliday *et al.*, 1964). This work has been continued, among others, by Gregory and Carroll (1979). Further work, on both register and genre, is currently being done in the Linguistics Department at Sydney University, particularly by Jim Martin.

Whereas sentences can be shown to be formed on the basis of knowledge of grammatical rules, texts arise on the basis of knowledge of rules and of exigencies which are first and foremost social in their nature — and in their functions and effects. In such a view of language, syntactic ability is significant and important, but it is regarded as facilitative and hence secondary to abilities which are in the first place social. That is to say, the ability to construct texts, alone or in conjunction with others, is seen to arise in response to social demands, which reflect the circumstances in which speakers or writers are placed, as well as their social needs and intentions. At the same time, this view of language has to be fully attentive to the fact that such abilities are distributed in line with the organizations resulting from social structures. In the case of western technological society that means they are distributed quite unevenly, along lines of class, gender, race, and other power-laden factors.

Linguistic maturity and linguistic development therefore are not finite, bounded or unitary concepts; there is not a single fixed set of categories which constitutes 'linguistic maturity', nor is there one process which constitutes 'linguistic development'. Rather, both are variable, dependent on the social history and present social place of any given individual, as well as on the character of the social structures in which he or she is located. For certain individuals linguistic development comes to its close relatively early in their lives — for instance, after their completed absorption into their place of work, achievement of parenthood, and integration into other relevant social groupings and situations. For other individuals linguistic development proceeds for a much longer period, associated say, with relatively significant job and/or class, and/or geographical mobility. It is not hard to see that, for some people, linguistic development is a near life-long process, and consequently linguistic maturity is long deferred. One thing is very clear, linguistic development proceeds right through the whole period of formal education, and linguistic maturity is certainly not reached at any point during that time.

If this view is correct, it has important implications for educational practice. At the simplest level, it means that a purely syntactically oriented view of language and of language education — with all its attendant paraphernalia of syntactic measurements, has to be drastically rethought. Furthermore, there can be no question of attempting to reach and teach 'linguistic maturity' as a finite, unitary and homogeneous entity within the period of primary, secondary or even tertiary education. Most importantly, linguistic development and linguistic maturity must be reconsidered as the *social* constructs that they, in fact, are. That is, linguistic maturity and linguistic development have to be seen in terms of the social structures into and through which children will move and of the social demands of those structures. Seen, in other words, in terms of political issues such as the possibility of social mobility for the individual and the possibility of social change, or conversely the wish for social stability and preservation of the status quo.

I am not of course saying that educators have not always considered such issues, nor that certain educational thinking about language has not been along these lines. I am saying that, in the mainstream of linguistic theorizing and in the mainstream of educational policies on language, the effects of such thinking have not made themselves felt. Perhaps, in part, this has been because the linguistic groundwork did not exist, but perhaps, in part, because of the highly political aspects of such practices. In the following sections of this paper I wish to sketch out some of the important notions underlying such a view, and thereby to suggest possible courses of action in language education.

Discourse, Genre and Text

The first question that presents itself within the view of language just sketched out is: 'How do texts come about?' We know something about the rules which are implemented in the production of smaller linguistic units — phrases, clauses, intonational units, clause-complexes, sentences. We also know something about the grammatical inventories and potential of particular languages — about transitivity types, tense forms and modality options, and we are beginning to understand how smaller level linguistic units are integrated into larger texts. We know next to nothing about the kinds of texts current within a given social structure at a given time, nor about their functions, their forms, meanings and constraints. We have little idea how larger scale social factors act to marshal the smaller scale linguistic features into coherent texts. What is it that gives rise to the systematic selection of linguistic features, and what is it that gives texts their varied but nevertheless predictable forms? The two terms which I will use here to pursue these questions are *discourse* and *genre*.

The meanings and structures of a particular social formation give rise to specific forms of language — to specific modes of talking or writing about those social and cultural aspects which are, centrally or marginally, of significance to a social group. It is these 'modes of talking' which I refer to as *discourse*. My use of the term draws heavily on the work of Michel Foucault (1971 and 1980). I am also drawing on the ideas of Voloshinov (1973) and consider his book contains by far the best discussion of the whole area of discourse from a linguistic point of view.

The meaning I attach to the term *discourse* is quite specific, and not at all to be confused with other uses of that term, in particular with the use which means 'any extended piece of language'. Here its meaning is close to that in such usages as 'sexist discourse', 'legal discourse', 'racist discourse', 'medical discourse', etc. In essence the term points to the fact that social institutions produce specific ways of writing or talking about certain areas of social life which are related to the place and nature of that institution. That is to say, in relation to certain areas of social life which are of particular significance to an institution, the institution will produce a set of statements which largely define, describe, delimit, and circumscribe what it is possible and impossible to say with respect to that area, and therefore how it is to be talked and written about. For example, matters such as gender, race, authority, professionalisms, science and family structures all have specific discourses associated with them. Each of these discourses circumscribes the possible ways of talking and writing in relation to specific topics. Sexist discourse, for instance, determines how men and women are to see themselves and how they are to be seen, what men and women may or may not do, as well as how their interactions are to be structured in terms of power. Indeed, as is now well enough documented, the prescriptions of sexist discourse extend to the family, the workplace and permeate all central areas of social life, both public and private.

I now want to consider a brief example, without overmuch analysis, from medical discourse. I wish to indicate how the structures of medical institutions, in this case psychiatry, find their expression in the discourse, constructing in the process the categories of patient, of specific diseases, and of the cure. Further, I wish to show briefly how this particular mode of language determines the appearance of specific linguistic forms and categories, and acts in the constitution of a text. The text cited is part of a ten-page pamphlet describing uses and effects of a drug used in the treatment of schizophrenia. My analysis is based on the theory put forward in *Language as Ideology* (Kress, and Hodge, 1979). Further descriptions of texts, based on this theory, can be found in *Language and Control* (Fowler, *et al.*, 1979).

Fluphenazine

The System of Schizophrenia Management — The long-acting injectable specific for and uniquely suited to the problems of schizopherenic patients.

Modecate (fluphenazine decanoate)

For assured long-term maintenance of: (5)
The Unreliable Tablet Taker
'Approximately 20 per cent of all hospitalized inpatients, even under clinical supervision, sequester their medication.'
'Approximately 50 per cent of all discharged psychiatric patients fail to take even the first dose of the medication'. (10)
Goldberg, H.L. Di Mascio, A. Chaudhary, B.: Psychosomatics 11:173, May-June, 1970.

[] Suspect this problem if the patient has a poor response, a history of repeated hospitalizations, discontinuing medication or resistance to follow-up care. (15)
[] Prevent this problem with Modecate when the patient's continued well-being depends on uninterrupted therapy.
[] Anticipate fewer hospitalizations, fewer days in the hospital with Modecate therapy.

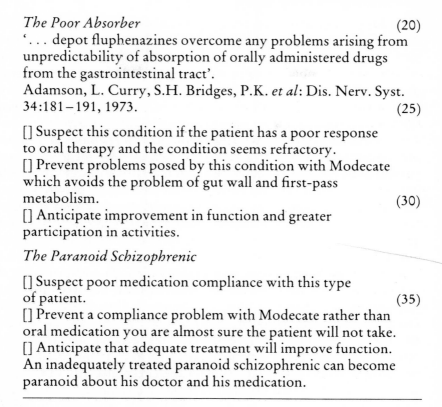

The Poor Absorber (20)

'. . . depot fluphenazines overcome any problems arising from
unpredictability of absorption of orally administered drugs
from the gastrointestinal tract'.

Adamson, L. Curry, S.H. Bridges, P.K. *et al*: Dis. Nerv. Syst.
34:181–191, 1973. (25)

[] Suspect this condition if the patient has a poor response
to oral therapy and the condition seems refractory.

[] Prevent problems posed by this condition with Modecate
which avoids the problem of gut wall and first-pass
metabolism. (30)

[] Anticipate improvement in function and greater
participation in activities.

The Paranoid Schizophrenic

[] Suspect poor medication compliance with this type
of patient. (35)

[] Prevent a compliance problem with Modecate rather than
oral medication you are almost sure the patient will not take.

[] Anticipate that adequate treatment will improve function.
An inadequately treated paranoid schizophrenic can become
paranoid about his doctor and his medication.

The text contains a number of features which are characteristic of
general scientific discourse, of western medical discourse, and of
psychiatric discourse. The tendency towards classification is strongly
marked: patients are classified as *unreliable tablet takers* (lines 6),
poor absorbers (line 20) and *paranoid schizophrenics* (line 33) (and
elsewhere as *dependable tablet takers*). These classificational terms
describe and are derived from the perceived symptoms of patients.
They become the names of patients, so that patients are named after
their symptoms or disease. In the course of this naming the disease
becomes focal and the patient, as human being, may recede to the
blurred margins of perception.

This process of depersonalization is a characteristic of medical
discourse and manifests itself here in other syntactic features. For
instance, actions which are in fact performed by patients are presented in a linguistic form which makes them appear as separated
from them, presents them as independent objective entities, which are
then (re-) attached to the patient as a disease or symptom from which
he or she suffers. Examples here are: 'prevent a *compliance problem*'

(line 36) — instead of 'prevent the patient from failing to comply' and 'suspect *poor medication compliance*' (line 34) — rather than 'suspect that the patient complies poorly with medication'. Further, actions which are not under the direct control of the patient are presented syntactically in the same way as those which are, so that the effect of a lack of control by the patient is further increased; for instance terms such as *unpredictability of absorption*, (line 22) and *improvement in function*, (line 31) which describe involuntary physiological processes are syntactically equivalent to terms such as *poor medication compliance* (line 34) which describe voluntary processes. Through this syntactic equation and elimination of the distinction between voluntary and involuntary processes all processes come to seem automatic and beyond the patient's control. Hence the patient ceases to be seen as an active (and responsible) causer of events, with the result that agency and causation pass to the doctor and to the drug. (Note, however, that an alternative way of describing patients is used in the quotations from the first of the two medical reports cited, i.e.: 'inpatients ... sequester their medication', [lines 7–8] and 'discharged patients fail to take even the first dose,' [lines 9–10]). A range of other linguistic forms reinforces this general depersonalizing tendency. For instance, one prominent form is a construction with the possessive *has* : 'the patient has a poor response' (line 13) instead of 'the patient responds poorly', again taking agency from the person and replacing it by a construction which replaces process by symptom and attaches that to the person as an attribute.

However brief and sketchy, the analysis does point to significant features of this discourse which have to do with the institution of psychiatric medicine, its practices and its structures — its attitudes towards human beings as well as notions of disease and of treatment. Psychiatric discourse, like discourse in general, does not merely passively reflect the 'real world'. Rather, it is an active constituent in the practices and structures which constitute and maintain that world; it has material effects. Medical discourse thus provides not only a mode of talking about an area of social life; it is implicated in every aspect of thinking, being, and doing with respect to this area. The possibility of transformation from named human being with some dignity and responsibility, to patient, then to 'the poor absorber in Ward 5' is just one example of very real, material effects.

Discourse by itself does not constitute texts. That is, while the mode of talking or writing provides the operative categories in the formation of texts, it does not determine the form that texts will assume. That form is provided by a particular *genre*. At any point in the history of a social group there exists a repertoire of linguistic textual forms, spoken and written. These are the genres which determine the textual form in which a specific discourse finds its expression. Genres are intimately tied into the social, political and cultural structures and practices of a given society, and arise as expressions of certain fundamental meanings of these structures and practices. In other words, textual genres are themselves not simply empty vessels but enshrine specific social meanings.

Each genre has its own formal, textual character though the formal structures of most of these genres are not well understood. Very little research indeed has been done in this field, with the exception of certain, mainly literary genres — for instance, we do know what the formal properties of sonnets are and we have some idea of the formal properties of short stories and novels. Some study, however, has been done of non-literary genres. These include the genre of the scientific paper (Hutchins, 1977) of interviews (Fowler, *et al.*, 1979) of classroom lessons (Sinclair and Coulthard, 1975) and of pupil group discussions (Barnes and Todd, 1977). Each of these genres shows adherence to strict, formal structural criteria, quite as strict as those of say, the Shakespearian sonnet. From this we know that textual forms are conventional, therefore are learned — that they are social and carry social meaning.

Anyone who reads or writes papers for a scientific journal will know that there are very precise rules to be followed in the construction of a text within that genre. It is equally well known that the formal requirements of this genre are absolutely tied into and arise out of the practices of the institution of science, and hence are expressions of the meanings of that institution. As remarked above genres are not merely empty forms available and waiting to be filled with content; rather they have specific meanings and they produce quite specific material effects. That is why 'being scientific' or 'being a scientist' has as much to do with, and is defined as much by, mastery and implementation of the requisite genres as it has to do with any of the other practices that constitute modern science. Effects of factualness or non-factualness are produced by the formal structures of genres: so, for example, the genre of the scientific paper or of a newspaper editorial produces the former, while the genre of the novel or of casual gossip produces the latter.

Genres are also selective and specific in another sense. As I have pointed out, a given genre conveys a certain set of meanings. At the same time, any one genre selects the *range* of things that may be said within its form. The genres of newspaper editorial, of scientific paper, or of Shakespearian sonnet demonstrate this point equally well. Only matters of public concern, and of a certain level of seriousness, are normally talked about in the newspaper editorial. The question of Uncle Fred's sexual proclivities cannot be talked about in a scientific paper. Until Milton wrote his sonnets the overt discussion of politics was not a fit subject matter for that genre in English. This last point illustrates, incidentally, that the relation of genre and subject-matter is not fixed, but is a matter for socially conditioned change.

Texts then are constructs produced in the relatively constrained interrelation of discourse — the way of talking on a given matter — and of genre — the formal structure which gives the text its material form. To use the somewhat homely analogy of cooking (with all the problems of homely analogies): discourse is akin to a category that describes and provides the range of permissible foodstuffs within a cultural grouping (i.e., ways of talking/thinking about the socio-cultural area of food); genre is like that category which describes and provides the range of socially permissible recipes. Texts, to extend the analogy, would be the equivalent of dishes and meals and the role of syntax would be akin to the knowledge involved in the smaller routines of cooking — boiling, braising, deep-frying, simmering, peeling, slicing, etc. A view of language which focuses on and equates general linguistic maturity with full proficiency in syntactic abilities alone is thus akin to a view of cooking which holds that to be a chef consists in the ability, say, to peel an onion and boil it.

Texts in Interaction

So far I have discussed text outside of the context of interaction, and by implication suggested that texts come about through the actions of single individuals, that is to say, are the work of single authors. Instead of the term 'voice' I use the term author, partly because 'voice' has a long history and very specific meanings in the discourse of literary theory (more so than the term author) and partly because the literary use of 'voice' includes aspects of what I treat here as matters of discourse and of genre. A further reason is to make connections with recent structuralist and post-structuralist work on the notion of author.

In fact, all texts have multiple authorship. This is most obvious in the case of interviews, discussions, idle talk, jointly written reports, papers, books, scripts and so on. In these instances a number of people are known and can be seen to have contributed, more or less unequally, to the construction of such texts. Multiple authorship is less obvious in other cases, for instance in a report in a newspaper. This may have all the appearance of having been written by a single author and sometimes it may appear with the name of a journalist/ author against it. Nevertheless we know that a whole chain of 'authors' has been involved in the construction of the text. There may have been the government spokesperson (who usually 'reports' or 'presents' what other authors may have said), the reporter who makes 'an account' of that text for a press-agency, the journalist who 'writes' a report from the agency's telex, the sub-editor who 'edits' the report in accord with the various demands of sub-editing. Each of these contributes in some measure, always significantly, to the final form of the text, adding, subtracting, condensing, expanding and always transforming. A detailed analysis of such multiple authorship is given in Trew's 'Theory at work' in *Language and Control* (Fowler, *et al.*, 1979). There is, indeed a large literature on the notion of author and an important initial text in the debate is 'The death of the author' (Barthes, 1977), another is 'What is an author?' (Foucault, 1979). Examples of recent treatments of the notions of text, reader and author can be found respectively in: Young (1981); Norris (1982) and Belsey (1980).

If all the authors of such multiple texts come from within the same social group, occupying the same place in the social group, occupying the same place in the social structure, they will also use the same discourse. In fact, however, this is most unlikely to be the case. In the case of the news report, it is more likely that speakers from very different social groups, and occupying different social places, will be the authors in the chain mentioned. Consequently some or all of these authors will speak about the issue at hand from within differing discourses. The resultant text is therefore a construct arising out of the interaction of differing discourses — competing, contradicting and jostling for domination. That is, each author in turn will attempt to appropriate the text to the discourse within which he or she feels the topic needs to be dealt with and thus to rewrite it in terms of the categories of a specific discourse. In the course of such successive rewriting traces of all these discourses remain in the text, and the text consequently is like an archaeological site of competing discourses. A successful author is one who (re)writes the text in such a way that the inconsistencies, incongruities and contradictions disappear from the surface of the text, or at least do not become obtrusive for a casual reader.

Gunther Kress

The co-presence of a number of discourses in the same text is the rule rather than the exception. At times this is a matter of the co-presence of contradictory discourses, at other times it is a matter of the co-presence of discourses which provide alternative though not necessarily contradictory accounts within a specific area. Where multiple authorship is overt, as in the texts of interviews, discussions, co-authored books or papers, discourse differences are likely to be more apparent, and the contest of the domination by one discourse over another may become the core of the text's constitution. However, given that individuals participate in a variety of social groups, occupy various social positions and frequently have complex social histories, then even those texts which do seem to have single authorship involve all the differences and contradictions of which the social experience of any one individual consists. More than that, all texts draw on a vast range of other texts, and on the discourses which have led to their constitution. These are the texts which writers themselves have experienced, and which in their turn have drawn on other texts in the same way. Each act of speaking and writing is thus placed in a vast web of previous writing and speaking so that texts are constructs which entail innumerable relations in a vast mesh of intertextuality. In other words, texts always bear the signs of the varying discourses which operate within a given social group and of other texts which have been their historical antecedents, or which have currency and significance at the moment of the new text's construction.

Texts which arise in interaction also bear the signs of the power differences which exist between the participants in the interaction. Differences in social power affect text in two ways. On the one hand the discourse of the participant with greatest social power is likely to dominate the text, so that the history of the text's construction is at the same time a record of the differential power of the various participants. That is to say, the categories of the discourse of the powerful will dominate such texts. Where power is more equally distributed between the participants, the text becomes the record of genuine contest and at times of adaptation and change in discourse organization — even if only for the duration of that particular text.

On the other hand, texts also bear the signs of power difference more directly, to the extent that nearly all aspects of language serve to express the power-relations between participants in an interaction. Detailed descriptive analyses of the expression of power in language can be found in *Language as Ideology* (Kress and Hodge, 1979) and in *Language and Control* (Fowler *et al.*, 1979). These matters are usually discussed in terms of 'politeness', 'hesitation', 'timidity' etc., when in fact they are an expression of power or lack of power, very precisely and rigidly coded. These are matters which must be learned and are an absolutely essential and integral part of linguistic maturity.

Public and Private Discourse: Speech and Writing

Discourses arise out of the nature of social institutions as expressions of their meanings. In turn discourses are effective factors in the constitution of those institutions and of individuals within them. Hence, because power is unequally distributed within societies and between social institutions, certain discourses will clearly be bearers of greater power than other discourses. This fact at once ranges both the modes of talking and the users of discourse in a hierarchy of power. In particular, the meanings of powerful institutions and of their discourses are accorded certain social relevance and prominence, and their meanings are accorded the status of knowledge in the public sphere. Conversely, the meanings associated with relatively powerless institutions and their discourses are not accorded such status. Hence these do not emerge into the public sphere and do not attain the status of public knowledge. Access to social power and to social effectiveness in the public sphere is thus tied in with and regulated through and by discourse. It follows that access to and command of specific discourses, and of their associated linguistic genres, is thus an absolute pre-requisite to full social effectiveness.

In western technological societies this distinction is further coded in the differences between the two modes of language, speech and writing. I have discussed this issue in a paper called 'The Social Values of Speech and Writing' (in Kress and Hodge, 1979) and more recently in 'Learning to Write' (Kress, 1982). Hoggart's (1952) 'The Uses of Literacy' is an important earlier work, and so is 'The Consequences of Literacy' (Goody and Watt, 1972).

Writing, characteristically, is the mode of public discourses; speech, equally characteristically, is the mode of private discourses. These two modes of language have fundamentally differing grammatical and textual/generic organizations,, which in their turn code and give expression to some of the crucial meanings of public and private discourses. These organizations have to do with fundamentally differing logics, with differing conceptions of the place of speakers/ writers in a social structure, and in relation to their audience. They also have to do with differing cognitive orientations and potentials, and differing attitudes to knowledge and to the creation, dissemination, control and ownership of knowledge. Just as command of powerful and public discourses is a pre-requisite for full social effectiveness, so a full command of the written mode of language is an absolutely essential requirement for effective participation in the public sphere. Given that the written mode is the mode of power and of public life, it is to be expected that its forms will intrude upon and even govern the speech of those who wish to assert, emphasize or maintain their power. Hence the spoken language of the more powerful is characteristically marked by the syntactic textual and generic forms of the written mode. The speech of the less powerful, which is not marked in this way, thus appears doubly powerless: powerless because it is initially the mode of the relatively powerless private domain, and made to seem even more so by contrast with the speech of the powerful which is, in reality, the written mode being used in speech.

As I mentioned at the beginning of this paper, the linguistic development of an individual is entirely tied in with the social and cultural experiences of that individual. While he or she experiences new social situations, assumes new places in the same or in a new social structure, he or she will necessarily experience linguistic development. Linguistic maturity represents the point when the speaker or writer has achieved full effectiveness in these terms, that is, within the range of socio-cultural needs and demands of a given group. Linguistic maturity does not, therefore, equate with effectiveness in all areas of the life of a society. A particular problem here is an often unacknowledged sliding between the two terms 'linguistic maturity' and 'linguistic adequacy'. The concept of 'linguistic adequacy' is fraught with enormous linguistic, social and political difficulties; it has been hugely detrimental to serious discussion of this general area.

It may well be an educational and a political goal to make it possible for all individuals to achieve full effectiveness in the public spheres of their society, to enable them to exercise power as fully effective members of society at large. Indeed, it seems to me that this must be a fundamental goal of any education system in a democratic society. Given the inequalities of power, however, it is also unlikely to be achieved. Consequently it is absolutely essential that linguistic maturity as such should not be equated with this particular goal. If it is, all those who do not participate (and exercise power) in the public domain would not only be excluded from full social effectiveness but would be further stigamatized as linguistically immature. That is, in fact, not unlike the situation of many of our fellow citizens at the moment. One worthwhile goal of a language curriculum might be the elimination of such injustice.

Linguistic Development, Linguistic Maturity and Language Education

In the preceding sections, I have attempted to sketch, in rough outline, some of the major factors that are effective in the constitution of texts. First and foremost, texts are the material forms of the expression and interplay of the social category of discourse. Hence an understanding of the social nature of discourse and of its social effects is absolutely essential in any programme of language education. Linguistic development is dependent on that, and on an understanding of the meanings of the discourses which are most important and effective for and in the social group of the individual. Linguistic maturity requires such understanding and involves the ability to control discourse for the purposes of the speaker or writer. It entails a full understanding and effective control of these factors *in interaction*; a knowledge of the linguistic forms and effects of power, and of their effective implementation in the construction of texts. A linguistically mature individual needs to have effective control of the genres and the modes of language in which the significant discourses of his or her group find expression.

No language curriculum can hope to give students knowledge and mastery of all the discourses and of all the generic forms of even one social group. It certainly cannot give them experience of all aspects of power and of its effects in society. It can however make students aware of the fundamental nature of discourse and acquaint them with crucially important genres. It can point out the forms and effects of power and teach effectiveness in the mode of public discourse, that is, in writing. It can also value properly the forms, functions and potentials of the mode of private discourse, that is, of informal speech. In this way a language curriculum might become more nearly adequate to the realities of linguistic development, and give teachers and students alike an insight into the full range of abilities and practices implied in the term linguistic maturity.

General Bibliography

AHLBERG, A. and J. (1978) *Each Peach Pear Plum*, London, Methuen.

AINSWORTH, M.D.S., S.M. and STAYTON, D.J. (1974) 'Infant-mother attachment of social development: socialization as a product of reciprocal responsiveness to signals', in RICHARDS, P.M.P. (Ed.) *The Integration of a Child into a Social World*. Cambridge, Cambridge University Press.

ANDERSON, V., BEREITER, C. and SMART, D. (1980) *Activation of Semantic Networks in Writing: Teaching Students How to Do it Themselves*, paper presented at the Annual Meeting of the American Educational Research Association, Boston.

APPLEBEE, A.N. (1978) *The Child's Concept of Story: Ages Two to Seventeen*, London, University of Chicago Press.

AUSTIN, J.L. (1962) *How to Do Things With Words*, Oxford, Clarendon Press.

BAKHTIN, M.H. (1981) *The Dialogic Imagination*, Austin, Texas, University of Texas Press.

BARNES, D. (1969) 'Language in the secondary classroom' in BARNES, D., BRITTON, J., and ROSEN, H. *Language, the Learner, and the School*, Harmondsworth, Penguin.

BARNES, D. (1976) *From Communication to Curriculum*, Harmondsworth, Penguin.

BARNES, D. and SCHEMILT, D. (1974) 'Transmission and interpretation', *Educational Review*, 26, 3, pp. 213–28.

BARNES, D. and TODD, F. (1977) *Communication and Learning in Small Groups*, London, Routledge and Kegan Paul.

BARNES, S.B., GUTFREUND, M., SATTERLY, D.J. and WELLS, C.G. (1983) 'Characteristics of adult speech which predict children's language development'. *Journal of Child Language*, 10, pp. 65–84.

BARTHES, R. (1977) 'The death of the author', in HEATH, S. (Ed.) *Image Music Text*, London, Fontana.

BARTLETT, E.J. (1981) *Learning to Write: Some Cognitive and Linguistic Components*, WASHINGTON, D.C., Centre for Applied Linguistics, (now distributed through Harcourt, Brace and Jovanovitch).

BARTLETT, E.J. (1982) 'Learning to revise: Some component processes', in NYSTRAND, M. (Ed.) *What Writers Know*, New York, Academic Press.

BATES, E. and MACWHINNEY, B. (1982) 'Functionalist approaches to grammar', in WANNER, E. and GLEITMAN, L.R. (Eds.) *Language Acquisition*, Cambridge, Cambridge University Press.

BATESON, G. (1973) *Steps to an Ecology of Mind*, St. Albans, England, Grenada Publishing Company.

BELLACK, A., KLIEBARD. H., HYMAN, R., and SMITH, F. (1966) *The Language of the Classroom*, New York, Teachers' College Press.

BELLUGI, U. and BROWN, R. (Eds.) (1964) 'The acquisition of language'. *Monographs of the Society for Research in Child Development*, 29, 1.

BELSEY, C. (1980) *Critical Practice*, London, Methuen.

BENNETT, N. *et al.* (1976) *Teaching Style and Pupil Performance*, London, Open Books.

BENNETT, N. and DESFORGES, C. (1984) *The Quality of Pupil Learning Experiences*, Hillsdale, New Jersey, Lawrence Erlbaum.

BEREITER, C. (1980) 'Development in writing', in GREGG, L.W. and STEINBERG, E.R. (Eds.) *Cognitive Processes in Writing*, Hillsdale, New Jersey, Lawrence Erlbaum Associates.

BEREITER, C. (1984) this volume, Chapter 6.

BEREITER, C., BAIRD, W. and SCARDAMALIA, M. (1981) 'Planning for rhetorical goals', paper presented at the Annual Meeting of the American Educational Research Association, Los Angeles.

BEREITER, C. and SCARDAMALIA, M. (1982) 'From conversation to composition: the role of instruction in a developmental process', in GLASER, R. (Ed.) *Advances in Instructional Psychology*, 2, Hillsdale, New Jersey, Lawrence Erlbaum Associates.

BEREITER, C. and SCARDAMALIA, M., in press, 'Cognitive coping strategies and the problem of "inert knowledge"', in CHIPMAN, S.S. *et al.* (Eds.) *Thinking and Learning Skills*, 2, Hillsdale, New Jersey, Lawrence Erlbaum Associates.

BERGER, P.L. and LUCKMAN, T. (1966) *The Social Construction of Reality*, Harmondsworth, Penguin.

BERNSTEIN, B. (1971) *Class, Codes, and Control, 3. Towards a Theory of Educational Transmissions*, London, Routledge and Kegan Paul.

BERRY, M. (1980). 'Layers of exchange structure', *Discourse Analysis Monographs*, 7, University of Birmingham, English Language Research.

BEVERIDGE, M. (Ed.) (1983) *Children Thinking Through Language*, London, Arnold.

BISSEX, G. (1980) *GNYS AT WRK: A Child Learns to Write and Read*, Cambridge, Mass, Harvard University Press.

BLOOM, L. (1970) *Language Development: Form and Function in Emerging Grammars*, Cambridge, Massachusets, MIT Press.

BOWERMAN, M. (1982) 'Re-organizational processes in language development', in WANNER, E. and GLEITMAN, L.R. (Eds.) *Language Acquisition*, Cambridge, Cambridge University Press.

BRITTON, J.N. (1970) *Language and Learning*, Harmondsworth, Penguin.

BRITTON, J. 1971 'What's the use — a schematic account of language function', *Educational Review*, 23, 3, pp. 205–19.

BRITTON, J. *et al.* (1975) *The Development of Writing Abilities 11 to 18*, London, Macmillan.

BRITTON, J. (1984) *Prospect and Retrospect*, London, Heinemann.

BRONFENBRENNER, U. (1974) *Is Early Intervention Effective?*, Washington, D.C., Department of Health, Education and Welfare.

BROWN, R. (1958) *Words and Things*, Glencoe, Illinois, Free Press.

BROWN, R. (1973) *A First Language: The Early Stages*, Cambridge, Mass, Harvard University Press and London, Allen and Unwin.

BROWN, R. and BELLUGI, R. (1964) 'Three processes in the child's acquisition of syntax', *Harvard Educational Review*, 34, pp. 131–51.

BRUNER, J.S. (1975) 'The ontogenesis of speech acts', *Journal of Child Language* 2, pp. 1–20.

BRUNER, J.S. (1981) 'The pragmatics of acquisition', in DEUTSCH, W. (Ed.) *The Child's Construction of Language*, London, Academic Press.

BRUNER, J.S., VOLLY, A. and SYLVA, K. (Eds.) (1976) *Play*, Harmondsworth, Penguin.

BULLOWA, M. (Ed.) (1979) *Before Speech: The Beginnings of Human Communication*, Cambridge, Cambridge University Press.

BURTIS, P.J., BEREITER, C., SCARDAMALIA, M. and TETROE, J. (1983) 'The development of planning in writing', in KROLL, B. and WELLS, C.G. (Eds.) *Exploration in the Development of Writing*, London, John Wiley.

CALKINS, L., McC., (1980) 'When children want to punctuate: Basic skills belong in context', *Language Arts* 57, pp. 567–73.

CAREY, S. (1978) 'The child as word learner', in HALLE, M. *et al.* (Eds.) *Linguistic Theory and Psychological Reality*, Cambridge, Mass, MIT Press.

CASE, R. (1978) 'Intellectual development from birth to adulthood: A neo-Piagetian interpretation', in SIEGLER, R.S. (Ed.) *Children's Thinking*, Hillsdale, New Jersey, Lawrence Erlbaum Associates.

CATTANI, C., SCARDAMALIA, M. and BEREITER, C. (1982) 'Facilitating diagnosis in student writing' paper presented at American Educational Research Association, New York.

CAZDEN, C.B. (1968) 'The acquisition of noun and verb inflections', *Child Development* 39, 2, pp. 433–48.

CAZDEN, C.B. (1973) 'Problems for education: Language as curriculum content and learning environment', in HAUGEN, E. and BLOOMFIELD, M. (Eds.) *Language as a Human Problem*, New York, W.W. Norton.

CAZDEN, C.B. (1976) 'Play with language and metalinguistic awareness', in BRUNER, J.S. *et al. Play*, Harmondsworth, Penguin.

CENTRAL ADVISORY COUNCIL FOR EDUCATION (1959) *15 to 18, Volume One* ('The Crowther Report') London, HMSO.

CENTRAL ADVISORY COUNCIL FOR EDUCATION (1963) *Half Our Future* ('The Newsom Report') London, HMSO.

CENTRAL ADVISORY COUNCIL FOR EDUCATION (1967) *Children and Their Primary Schools (The Plowden Report) Volume 1*, London, HMSO.

CHIPMAN, S.S., SEGAL, J.W. and GLASER, R. (Eds.) (in press.) *Thinking and Learning Skills: Current Research and Open Questions*, 2, Hillsdale, New Jersey, Lawrence Erlbaum Associates.

CHOMSKY, C. (1969) *The Acquisition of Syntax in Children from Five to Ten*, Cambridge, Mass., MIT Press.

CHOMSKY, N.A. (1959) 'Review of "Verbal Behaviour"' by B.F. SKINNER. *Language*, 35.

CHOMSKY, N.A. (1964) 'Discussion of Miller and Ervin Tripp's paper, in BELLUGI, U. and BROWN, R. (Eds.) *The Acquisition of Language*, Monographs of the Society for Research in Child-Development, 29, 1.

CHOMSKY, N.A. (1965) *Aspects of the Theory of Syntax*, Cambridge, Mass, MIT Press.

CHOMSKY, N.A. (1976) *Reflections on Language*, London, Temple Smith (in association with Fontana Books).

CHUKOVSKY, K. (1963) *From Two to Five*, Berkeley, California, University of California Press.

CICIRELLI, V.G., GRANGER, R.L. *et al.* (1969) *The Impact of Headstart Volume 1*, Washington, D.C., Westinghouse Learning Corporation and Ohio University.

CLARK, E. (1983) 'The young word maker; a case study of innovation in the child's lexicon', in WANNER, E. and GLIETMAN, L.R. (Eds.) *Language Acquisition*, Cambridge, Cambridge University Press.

CLAY, M.M. (1983) 'Getting a theory of writing', in KROLL, B. and WELLS, C.G. (Eds.) *Exploration in the Development of Writing*, London, John Wiley.

COULTHARD, M. and BRAZIL, D. (1979) 'Exchange structure', *Discourse Analysis Monographs*, 5, University of Birmingham, English Language Research.

COULTHARD, M. and MONTGOMERY, M. (1981) 'Originating a description' in COULTHARD, M. and MONTGOMERY, M. (Eds.) *Studies in Discourse Analysis* London, Routledge and Kegan Paul.

CRAGO, H. and M. (1983) *Prelude to Literacy: A Pre-school Child's Encounter with Picture and Story*, Carbondale, Illinois, Southern Illinois University Press.

CROMER, R.F. (1979) 'The strengths of the weak form of the cognition hypothesis for language acquisition', in LEE, V. (Ed.) *Language Development*, London, Croom Helm.

CRONNELL, B. (1980) *Punctuation and Capitalisation: A Review of the Literature*, Los Alamitos, California, South West Regional Laboratory, Technical Note 2–80/27, November, (ED 208404)

CROSS, T.G. (1977) 'Mothers' speech adjustments: the contribution of selected child listener variables', in SNOW, C. and FERGUSON, C. (Eds.) *Talking to Children*, Cambridge, Cambridge University Press.

CROSS, T.G. (1978) 'Mothers' speech and its association with the rate of linguistic development in young children', in SNOW, C. and WATERSON, N. (Eds.) (1978) *The Development of Communication*, Cambridge, Cambridge University Press.

CUES, (1980) Inner London Education Authority, Centre for Urban Educational Studies *Listen, Discuss and Do Unit 4, Language for Learning* (revised edition) ILEA, Learning Resources Branch.

CULLER, J. (1975) *Structuralist Poetics*, London, Routledge and Kegan Paul.

CUMMINS, J. (1982) 'Mother Tongue Maintenance for Minority Language Children: some common misconceptions,' paper prepared for conference on Bilingualism and Education, Aberystwyth. Wales, September.

DARCY, N.T. (1963) 'Bilingualism and the Measurement of Intelligence: Review of a Decade of Research', *Journal of Genetic Psychology*, 3, pp. 259–82.

DAVIES, A. (Ed.) (1975) *Problems of Language and Learning*, London, Edward Arnold.

DEPARTMENT OF EDUCATION AND SCIENCE (1978) *Primary Education in England*, a survey by HM Inspectors of Schools, London, HMSO.

DEPARTMENT OF EDUCATION AND SCIENCE (1981) *Aspects of Secondary Education in England*, a survey by HM Inspectors of Schools, London, HMSO.

DEPARTMENT OF EDUCATION, NORTHERN IRELAND (1981) *Primary Education in Northern Ireland*, London, HMSO.

DES (1972) *Education: A Framework for Expansion*, London, HMSO.

DES (1975) *A Language for Life* ('The Bullock Report') London, HMSO.

DEUTSCH, W. (Ed.) (1981) *The Child's Construction of Language*, London, Academic Press.

DIXON, J. and STRATTA, L. (nd) 'Argument: what does it mean to teachers of English?', paper present for the Schools Council series *Achievement in Writing at 16+*.

DOMBEY, H. (1983) 'Learning the language of books', in MEEK, M. (Ed.) *Opening Moves*, Bedford Way Papers, London, University of London Institute of Education.

DONALDSON, M. (1966) 'Discussion of McNeill (1966) "The Creation of Language"', in LYONS, J. and WALES, R.J. (Eds.) *Psycho-Linguistic Papers*, Cambridge, Cambridge University Press.

DONALDSON, M. (1978) *Children's Minds*. London, Fontana.

DORE, J. (1975) 'Holophrases, speech acts and language universals,' *Journal of Child Language*, 2, pp. 21–40.

DORE, J. (1979) 'Conversation and pre-school language development' in FLETCHER, P. and GARMAN, M. (Eds.) *Language Acquisition*, Cambridge, Cambridge University Press.

DOUGHTY, P. *et al.* (1971) *Language in Use*, London, Arnold for Schools Council.

EAGLETON, T. (1983) *Literary Theory* Oxford, Blackwell.

EDELSKY, C. (1983) 'Segmentation and punctuation: developmental data from young writers in a bilingual programme', *Research in the Teaching of English*, 17, pp. 135–156.

EDWARDS, A. and FURLONG, V. (1978) *The Language of Teaching: Meaning in Classroom Interaction*, London, Heinemann.

EDWARDS, D. (1973) 'Sensory-motor intelligence and semantic relations in early child grammar', *Cognition*, 2, 4, pp. 395–434.

EMIG, J. (1981) 'Non-magical thinking: Presenting writing developmentally in schools', in FREDERICKSEN, C.H., WHITEMAN, M.F. and DOMINIC, J.F. (Eds.) *Writing*, 2, Hillsdale, New Jersey, Lawrence Erlbaum Associates.

ENGEL-CLOUGH, E. and DAVIES, P. with SUMNER, R.S. (1984) *Assessing Pupils: A Study of Practice*, London, NFER.

FATHMAN, A.K. (1976) 'Variables affecting the successful learning of English as a second language', *TESOL* Quarterly 10, 4, pp. 433–41.

FERGUSON, C. and SLOBIN, D.I. (Eds.) (1973) *Studies in Language Development*, New York, Holt Rinehart.

FERRIER, L. (1978) 'Some observations of error in context', in WATERSON, N. and SNOW, C. (Eds.) (1978) *The Development of Communication*, New York, John Wiley.

FILLMORE, C.J. (1968) 'The Case for Case', in BACH, E. and HARMS, R. (Eds.) *Universals in Linguistic Theory*, New York, Holt Rinehart.

FLETCHER, P. and GARMAN, M. (Eds.) (1979) *Language Acquisition*, Cambridge, Cambridge University Press.

FLOWER, L. (1979) 'Writer based prose: A cognitive basis for problems in writing', *College English*, 41, 1 September, pp. 19–37.

FLOWER, L. and HAYES, J.R. (1980a) 'The Cognition of discovery: defining a rhetorical problem', *College Composition and Communication*, 31, 2, pp. 21–32.

FLOWER, L. and HAYES, J.R. (1980b) 'The dynamics of composing: making plans and juggling constraints', in GREGG, L.W. and STEINBERG, E.R. (Eds.). *Cognitive Processes in Writing*, Hillsdale, New Jersey, Lawrence Erlbaum Associates.

FOUCAULT, M. (1971) 'Orders of discourse', *Social Science Information*, 10, 2, pp. 7–30.

FOUCAULT, M. (1979) 'What is an author?' *Screen*, 20, 1.

FOUCAULT, M. (1980) 'Prison Talk', in GORDON, C. (Ed.) *Power/Knowledge*, New York, Pantheon.

FOWLER, R., HODGE, R., KRESS, G. and TREW, T. (1979) *Language and Control*, London, Routledge and Kegan Paul.

FOX, C. (1983) 'Talking like a book, young children's early narrations', in MEEK, M. (Ed.) *Opening Moves*, Bedford Way Papers, 17, London, London University Institute of Education.

FOX, G. (Ed.) (1976) *Writers, Critics and Children*, London, Heinemann.

FREDERICKSEN, C.H., WHITEMAN, M.F. and DOMINIC, J.F. (Eds.) (1981) *Writing (Volume 2): Process, Development and Communication*, Hillsdale, New Jersey, Lawrence Erlbaum Associates.

FRENCH, P. and MACLURE, M. (1981) 'A comparison of talk at home and at school', in WELLS, C.G. (Ed.) *Learning Through Interaction: The Study of Language Development*, Cambridge, Cambridge University Press.

FRENCH, P. and WOLL, B. (1981) 'Context, meaning and strategy in parent-child conversation', in WELLS, C.G. (Ed.) *Learning Through Interaction: The Study of Language Development*, Cambridge, Cambridge University Press.

FURROW, D., NELSON, K. and BENEDICT, H. (1979) 'Mothers' speech to children and syntactic development: Some simple relationships', *Journal of Child Language*, 6, pp. 423–42.

GARVEY, C. (1975) 'Requests and responses in children's speech', *Journal of Child Language*, 2, pp. 41–6.

GIACOBBE, M.E. (1982) 'Who says children can't write the first weeks?' in WALSHE, R.D. (Ed.) *Donald Graves in Australia: Children Want to Write*, London, Heinemann.

GIGLIOLI, P.P. (Ed.) (1972) *Language and Social Context*, Harmondsworth, Penguin.

GILES, H., ROBINSON, W.P. and SMITH, P.M. (Eds.) (1980) *Language: Social and Psychological Perspectives*, Oxford, Pergamon.

GLASER, R. (Ed.) (1982) *Advances in Instructional Psychology*, 2, Hillsdale, New Jersey, Lawrence Erlbaum Associates.

GOODY, J. and WATT, I. (1972) 'The consequences of literacy', in GIGLIOLI, P.P. (Ed.) *Language and Social Context*, Harmondsworth, Penguin.

GORDON, C. (Ed.) (1980) *Power/Knowledge*, New York, Pantheon.

GRAVES, D.H. (1979) 'What children show us about revision', *Language Arts*, 56, 3, pp. 312–19.

GRAVES, D.H. (1983) *Writing: Teachers and Children at Work*, London, Heinemann.

GREENFIELD, P. (1980) 'Towards an operational and logical analysis of intentionality: the use of discourse in early child language', in OLSON, D. (Ed.) *The Social Foundations of Language and Thought*, New York, Norton.

GREGG, L.W. and STEINBERG, E.R. (Eds.) (1980) *Cognitive Processes in Writing*, Hillsdale, New Jersey, Lawrence Erlbaum Associates.

GREGORY, M. and CARROLL, S. (1979) *Language and Situation*, London, Routledge and Kegan Paul.

GRIFFITHS, M. and WELLS, C.G. (1983) 'Who writes what and why? in KROLL, B. and WELLS, C.G. (Eds.) *Explorations in the Development of Writing*, London, Wiley.

GRIFFITHS, P. (1979) 'Speech acts and early sentences', in FLETCHER, P. and GARMAN, M. (Eds.) *Language Acquisition*, Cambridge, Cambridge University Press.

HALLE, M., BRESNAN, J. and MILLER, G.A. (Eds.) (1978) *Linguistic Theory and Psychological Reality*, Cambridge, Mass, MIT, Press.

HALLIDAY, M. (1969) 'Relevant models of language', in *Education Review*, 22, 1, pp. 26–37.

HALLIDAY, M. (1974) *Language and Social Man*, London, Longmans.

HALLIDAY, M.A.K. (1975a) *Learning How to Mean*, London, Arnold.

HALLIDAY, M.A.K. (1975b) 'Talking one's way in: a sociolinguistic perspective on language and learning', in DAVIES, A. (Ed.) *Problems of Language and Learning*, London, Edward Arnold.

HALLIDAY, M.A.K. (1978) *Language as Social Semiotic*, London, Arnold.

HALLIDAY, M.A.K. and HASAN, R. (1976) *Cohesion in English*, London, Longman.

HALLIDAY, M.A.K., McINTOSH, A., and STREVENS, P. (1964) *The Linguistic Sciences and Language Teaching*, London, Longman.

HAMMERSLEY, M. (1977) 'School learning: the cultural resources used by pupils to answer a teacher's questions', in WOODS, P. and HAMMERSLEY, M. (Eds.) *School Experience*, London, Croom Helm.

HARGREAVES, D. (1984) *Improving Secondary Schools,* Inner London Education Authority.

HAUGEN, E. and BLOOMFIELD, M. (Eds.) (1973) *Language as a Human Problem*, New York, W. W. Norton.

HAWKINS, D. (1978) 'Critical barriers to science learning', *Outlook* 29 Autumn, pp. 3–25.

HAYES, J.R. and FLOWER, L. (1980) 'Identifying the organisation of writing processes', in GREGG, L.W. and STEINBERG, E.R. (Eds.) *Cognitive Processes in Writing*, Hillsdale, New Jersey, Lawrence Erlbaum Associates.

HEANEY, S. (1982) *Pre-occupations*, London, Faber.

HEATH, S. (1977) *Image Music Text*, London, Fontana.

HEATH, S.B. (1983) *Ways with Words*, Cambridge, Cambridge University Press.

HESTER, H. (1982) *Language in the Multi-ethnic Classroom*, (LIME) Video Programme 2, Inner London Education Authority, Learning Resources Branch.

HIDI, S. and HILDYARD, A. in press 'The comparison of oral and written productions of two discourse types'. *Discourse Processes*.

HOGGART, R. (1952) *The Uses Of Literacy*, Harmondsworth, Penguin.

HUGHES, S. (1983) 'Word and Image', Woodfield Lecture given at Loughborough University, England.

HUGHES, T. (1976) 'Myth and Education', in FOX, G. (Ed.) *Writers, Critics and Children*, London, Heinemann.

HUMAN RESOURCES RESEARCH ORGANIZATION (1977) *Guidebook for the Development of Army Training Literature*, Arlington, Virginia, US Army Research Institute for the Behavioural and Social Sciences.

HUNT, K.W. (1970) 'Syntactic maturity in school children and adults. *Monographs of the Society for Research in Child Development*, 35, 1, Chicago, University of Chicago Press.

HUTCHINS, J. (1977) 'On the Structure of Scientific Texts', *UEA Papers in Linguistics*, 5, Norwich, England, University of East Anglia.

HYMES, D. (1973) 'Speech and Language: on the origins and foundations of inequality among speakers', in HAUGEN, E. and BLOOMFIELD, M. (Eds.) *Language as a Human Problem*, Guildford, Lutterworth Press.

INNER LONDON EDUCATION AUTHORITY (1983) *Language Census*, Research and Statistics Branch, ILEA.

JOHNSON-LAIRD, P.N. and WASON, P.C. (Eds.) (1977) *Thinking*, Cambridge, Cambridge University Press.

KAYE, K. and CHARNEY, R. (1980) 'How mothers maintain dialogue with two year olds', in OLSON, D. (Ed.) *The Social Foundation of Language and Thought*, New York, Norton.

KRESS, G. (1982) *Learning to Write*, London, Routledge and Kegan Paul.

KRESS, G. and HODGE, R. (1979) *Language as Ideology*, London, Routledge and Kegan Paul.

KROLL, B. and WELLS, C.G. (Eds.) (1983) *Explorations in the Development of Writing*, London, John Wiley.

LABOV, W. (1970) 'The logic of non-standard English', in WILLIAMS, F. (Ed.) *Language and Poverty*, Chicago, Markham Publishing Company.

LABOV, W. (1972) *Language in the Inner City*, Philadelphia, University of Pennsylvania Press.

LACAN, J. (1977) *Ecrits*, London, Tavistock Press.

LEE, V. (Ed.) (1979) *Language Development*, London, Croom Helm.

LENNEBERG, E.H. (Ed.) (1964) *New Directions in the Study of Language*, Cambridge, Mass, MIT Press.

LENNEBERG, E.H. (1966) 'The natural history of language', in SMITH, F. and

MILLER, G.A. (Eds.) *The Genesis of Language*, MIT Press.

LMP/LINC (1983) *Report of the Linguistic Minorities Project, Linguistic Minorities in England*. London, University of London, Institute of Education.

LOCK, A. (Ed.) (1978) *Action, Gesture and Symbol: The Emergence of Language*, London, Academic Press.

LOCK, A. (1980) *The Guided Re-invention of Language*, London, Academic Press.

LUNZER, E. and GARDNER, K. (Eds.) (1979) *The Effective Use of Reading*, London, Heinemann.

LYONS, J. and WALES, R.J. (Eds.) (1966) *Psycholinguistic Papers*, Edinburgh, Edinburgh University Press.

MACKAY, D., THOMPSON, B. and SCHAUB, P. (1970) *Breakthrough to Literacy*, London, Longman for the Schools Council.

MACNAMARA, J. (1966) *Bilingualism and Primary Education*, Edinburgh, University of Edinburgh Press.

McCUTCHEN, D. and PERFETTI, C.A. (1982) 'Coherence and correctness in the development of discourse production', *Text*, 2, pp. 113–39.

McSHANE, J. (1980) *Learning to Talk*, Cambridge, Cambridge University Press.

McTEAR, M. (1981) 'Towards a model for the linguistic analysis of conversation' in *Belfast Working Papers in Language and Linguistics*, 5, pp. 79–92 Belfast, Ulster Polytechnic.

MANDL, H., STEIN, N. and TRABASSO, T. (Eds.) (in press) *Learning and Comprehension of Texts*, Hillsdale, New Jersey, Lawrence Erlbaum Associates.

MARTIN, N., DARCY, P., NEWTON, B. and PARKER, R. (1976) *Writing and Learning Across the Curriculum 11–16*, London, Ward Lock.

MARTLEW, M. (Ed.) (1983) *The Psychology of Written Language: A Developmental Approach*, London, John Wiley.

MEEK, M. (Ed.) (1983) 'Opening Moves' *Bedford Way Paper*, 17, London, University of London, Institute of Education.

MENYUK, P. (1969) *Sentences Children Use*, Cambridge, Mass, MIT Press.

MERCER, N. (1981) *Language in School and Community*, London, Arnold.

MINISTRY OF EDUCATION, BRITISH COLUMBIA (1979) *English as a Second Language for Vietnamese Students*, Curriculum Development Branch.

NELSON, K. (1973) 'Structure and strategy in learning to talk', *Monograph of the Society for Research in Child Development*, 38, 1–2, Serial No 149.

NEWPORT, E.L., GLEITMAN, H. and GLEITMAN, L.R. (1977) 'Mother I'd rather do it myself: Some effects and non-effects of maternal speech style', in SNOW, C.E. and FERGUSON, C.A. (Eds.) *Talking To Children*, Cambridge, Cambridge University Press.

NEWSON, J. (1978) 'Dialogue and development', in LOCK, A. (Ed.) *Action, Gesture and Symbol*, London, Academic Press.

NINIO, A. and BRUNER, J.S. (1978) 'The achievement and antecedents of labelling', *Journal of Child Language*, 5, pp. 1–16.

NOLD, E.W. (1981) 'Revising', in FREDERICKSEN, C.H. *et al.* (Eds.) *Writing*, 2, New Jersey, Lawrence Erlbaum Associates.

NORD, J.R. (1980) 'Developing Listening Fluency Before Speaking: an

Alternative Paradigm'. *System* 8, 1–22.

NORRIS, C. (1982) *Deconstruction*, London, Methuen.

NYSTRAND, M. (Ed.) (1982) *What Writers Know: The Language, Process and Structure of Written Discourse*, New York, Academic Press.

OLSON, D. (1977) 'From utterance to text: the bias of language in speech and writing'. *Harvard Educational Review* 47, 3, pp. 257–81.

OLSON, D. (Ed.) (1980) *The Social Foundations of Language and Thought*, New York, Norton.

OLSON, D. (Ed.) (in press) *The Cognitive Consequences of Literacy*, Cambridge, Cambridge University Press.

OPIE, I. and P. (1959) *The Lore and Language of School Children*, London, Oxford University Press.

PARIS, P. (1980) 'Discourse schemata as knowledge and as regulators of text production'. Unpublished Master's thesis, York University, Toronto, Ontario.

PEAL, E. and LAMBERT, W. (1962) 'Relation of bilingualism to intelligence', *Psychological Monographs* No. 546.

PHILLIPS, T. (1971) 'Poetry in the Junior School', *English in Education* 5, 3, pp. 51–62.

PHILLIPS, T. (1972) *Responsive-Reading: One Teacher's Approach*, Unit PE 951/6, Milton Keynes, The Open University.

PHILLIPS, T. (1975) 'After word to the group, the poem, and the individual' in *Children as Readers: Report to Schools Council*, Unpublished Schools Council Report (mimeo).

PHILLIPS, T. (1984) *The Analysis of Style in the Discourse of Middle School Children (10–12 years) Working in Small, Teacherless Groups*, Unpublished PhD thesis, Norwich, University of East Anglia.

PIAGET, J. and INHELDER, B. (1969) *The Psychology of the Child*, London, Routledge and Kegan Paul.

QUIRK, R. and GREENBAUM, S. (1973) *A University Grammar of English*, London, Longman.

READ, C. and SCHREIBER, P. (1982) 'Why short subjects are harder to find than long ones', in WANNER, E and GLEITMAN, L.R. (Eds.) *Language Acquisition*, Cambridge, Cambridge University Press.

RICHARDS, P.M.P. (Ed.) (1974) *The Integration of a Child into a Social World*, Cambridge, Cambridge University Press.

ROGERS, T. (Ed.) (1979) *These First Affections*, London, Routledge and Kegan Paul.

ROSCH, E. (1977) 'Classification of real-world objects: origins and representation in cognition', in JOHNSON-LAIRD, P.N. and WASON, P.C. (Eds.) *Thinking*, Cambridge, Cambridge University Press.

ROSEN, C. and ROSEN, H. (1973) *The Language of Primary School Children*, Harmondsworth, Penguin.

ROSEN, H. (1984) *Stories and Meanings*, London, National Association for the Teaching of English.

ROSEN, H. and BURGESS, T. (1980) *Languages and Dialects of London School Children*, London, Ward Lock.

ROSEN, M. and STEEL, S. (1983) *Inky Pinky Pouky*, London, Granada.

SARTRE, J.P. (1950) *What is Literature*, London, Methuen.

SAUNDERS, G. (1982) 'Bilingual Children: Guidance for the family', *Multilingual Matters*, 3, Clevedon, Avon, England.

SAVILLE-TROIKE, M. (1976) *Foundations for Teaching English as a Second Language*, New Jersey, Prentice Hall.

SCARDAMALIA, M. and BEREITER, C (1983) 'The development of evaluative, diagnostic and remedial capabilities in children's composing', in MARTLEW, M. (Ed.) *The Psychology of Written Language*, London, John Wiley.

SCARDAMALIA, M. and BEREITER, C. (in press) 'Development of strategies in text processing', in MANDL, H. *et al.* (Eds.) *Learning and Comprehension of Texts*, Hillsdale, New Jersey, Lawrence Erlbaum Associates.

SCARDAMALIA, M., BEREITER, C. and GOELMAN, H. (1982) 'The role of production factors in writing ability', in NYSTRAND, M. (Ed.) *What Writers Know*, New York, Academic Press.

SCARDAMALIA, M., BEREITER, C. and WOODRUFF, E. (1980) *The Effects of Content Knowledge on Writing*, paper presented at Annual Meeting of the American Educational Research Association, Boston.

SCARDAMALIA, M. and PARIS, P. (1982) 'The development of explicit discourse knowledge and its function in text representation and planning', Unpublished manuscript, York University, Toronto, Ontario.

SCHOOLS COUNCIL (1981) *The Practical Curriculum*, Working Paper No 70, London, Methuen.

SEARLE, J. (1969) *Speech Acts: An Essay in the Philosophy of Language*, Cambridge, Cambridge University Press.

SHATZ, M. (1982) 'On mechanisms of language acquisition: can features of the communicative environment account for development?' in WANNER, E. and GLEITMAN, L.R. (Eds.) *Language Acquisition*, Cambridge, Cambridge University Press.

SHIELDS, M. (1978) 'The child as psychologist: Construing the social world' in LOCK, A. (Ed.) *Action, Gesture and Symbol: The Emergence of Language*, London, Academic Press.

SHIELDS, M. (1980) *The Implications for Psychology of the Study of Dialogue Skills in Pre-school Children*, paper given to the Warsaw Academy of Science, London University Institute of Education, Department of Child Development (mimeo).

SIEGLER, R.S. (Ed.) (1978) *Children's Thinking: What Develops?* Hillsdale, New Jersey, Lawrence Erlbaum Associates.

SIEGLER, R.S. (1981) 'Developmental sequences within and between concepts'. *Monographs of the Society for Research in Child Development*, 46/2, Serial No 189.

SINCLAIR, J. and COULTHARD, M. (1975) *Towards an Analysis of Classroom Discourse: The English Used by Teachers and Pupils*, London, Oxford University Press.

SKINNER, B.F. (1957) *Verbal Behavior*, New York, Appleton.

SLOBIN, D.I. (1973) 'Cognitive prerequisites for the development of grammar', in FERGUSON, C. and SLOBIN, D.I. (Eds.) *Studies in Language Development*, New York, Holt Rinehart.

SLOBIN, D.I. (1979) *Psycholinguistics*, (2nd Edition), Glenview, Illinois, Scott Foresman.

SLOBIN, D.I. (1981) 'The origin of grammatical coding of events', in DEUTSCH, W. (Ed.) *The Child's Construction Language*, New York, Academic Press.

SLOBIN, D.I. (1982) 'Universal and particular in the acquisition of language', in WANNER, E. and GLEITMAN, L.R. (Eds.) *Language Acquisition*, Cambridge, Cambridge University Press.

SMITH, F. (1982) *Writing and the Writer*, New York, Holt, Rinehart and Winston.

SMITH, F. and MILLER, G.A. (1966) *The Genesis of Language*, MIT Press.

SNOW, C. and FERQUSON, C. (Eds.) (1977) *Talking to Children: Language Input and Acquisition*, Cambridge, Cambridge University Press.

SNOW, C. and WATERSON, N. (Eds.) (1978) *The Development of Communication*, New York, Wiley.

SOUTHGATE, V, ARNOLD, H. and JOHNSON, S. (1981) *Extending Beginning Reading*, London, Heinemann Educational, for Schools Council.

SOWERS, S. (1984) 'Learning to write in a workshop: A study in grades one through four', in FARR, M. (Ed.) *Advances in Writing Research Volume One: Children's early writing development*, Norwood, New Jersey, Ablex.

SPEIER, M. (1971) 'Some conversational problems for interactional analysis', in SUDNOW, D. (Ed.) *Studies in Interaction*, New York, Free Press.

SPEIER, M. (1976) 'The child as conversationalist: some culture-contact features of conversational interactions between adults and children's, in HAMMERSLEY, M. and WOODS, P. (Eds.) *The Process of Schooling: A Sociolinguistic Perspective*. London, Routledge and Kegan Paul.

SPENCER, M. (1976) 'Stories are for telling', *English in Education*, 10, 1, spring, pp. 16–23.

STATON, J. (1982) *Dialogue Journal Writing as a Communicative Event*, Washington, Centre for Applied Linguistics, Washington DC.

STEIN, N.L. and TRABASSO, T. (1982) 'What's in a story: An approach to comprehension and instruction', in GLASER, R. (Ed.) *Advances in Instructional Psychology*, 2, Hillsdale, New Jersey, Lawrence Erlbaum Associates.

STERN, D. (1977) *The First Relationship: Infant and Mother*, London, Open Books.

STUBBS, M. (1976a) 'Keeping in touch: some functions of teacher talk', in STUBBS, M. and DELAMONT, S. (Eds.) *Explorations in Classroom Observation*, London, Wiley.

STUBBS, M. (1976b) *Language, Schools and Classrooms*, London, Methuen.

SUDNEW, D. (Ed.) *Studies in Interaction*, New York, Free Press.

TANNEN, D. (1982) 'The oral/literate continuum in discourse', in TANNEN, D. (Ed.) *Spoken and Written Language: Exploring Orality and Literacy*, Norwood, New Jersey, Ablex.

TIZARD, B. (1974) 'Staff and Parent Talk to Young Children', in TIZARD, B. (Ed.) *Early Childhood Education*, Windsor, NFER Publishing Co.

TOUGH, J. (1973) *Focus on Meaning*, London, Allen and Unwin.

TREVARTHEN, C. (1979) 'Communication and co-operation in early infancy: A description of primary intersubjectivity', in BULLOWA, M. (Ed.) *Before Speech*, Cambridge, Cambridge University Press.

TREVARTHEN, C., and HUBLEY, R. (1978) 'Secondary intersubjectivity: confidence, confiding, and acts of meaning in the first year', in LOCK, A. (Ed.) *Action, Gesture and Symbol*, London, Academic Press.

TRUDGILL, P. (1975) *Accent, Dialect and the School*, London, Arnold.

URWIN, C. (1983) 'The contribution of non-visual communication systems and language to knowing oneself', in BEVERIDGE, M. (Ed.) *Children Thinking Through Language*, London, Arnold.

VAN DIJK, T. (1977) *Text and Context*, London, Longman.

VAN DIJK, T. (1979) 'Discourse studies in education', *Australian Review of Applied Linguistics*, 5.

VOLOSHINOV, V.N. (1973) *Marxism and the Philosophy of Language* (translated by MATEJKA, L. and TITUNIK, I.R.) London, Seminar Press.

VYGOTSKY, L.S. (1932) *Thought and Language*, Cambridge, Mass, MIT Press.

VYGOTSKY, L.S. (1933) 'Play and its role in the mental development of the child', in BRUNER, J.S. *et al.* (Eds.) (1976) *Play*, Harmondsworth Penguin.

VYGOTSKY, L.S. (1962) *Mind in Society*, Cambridge, Mass, MIT Press.

VYGOTSKY, L.S. (1977) *Thinking and Speech*, Selected passages of Myshlenie i Rech translated by SUTTON, A., Centre for Child Study, University of Birmingham.

VYGOTSKY, L.S. (1978) *Mind in Society*, Cambridge, Mass, Harvard University Press.

WALKERDINE, V. (1983) 'A psychosemiotic approach to abstract thought', in BEVERIDGE, M. (Ed.) *Children Thinking Through Language*, London, Arnold.

WALSHE, R.D. (Ed.) (1982) *Donald Graves in Australia: Children want to write*, London, Heinemann.

WANNER, E. and GLEITMAN, L.R. (Eds.) (1982) *Language Acquisition: The State of the Art*, Cambridge, Cambridge University Press.

WARNOCK, M. (1978) *Special Educational Needs*. Report of the Committee of Enquiry into the Education of Handicapped Children and Young People ('The Warnock Report') London, HMSO.

WATERSON, N. and SNOW, C. (Eds.) (1978) *The Development of Communication*, New York, John Wiley.

WEAVER, C. (1982) 'Welcoming errors as signs of growth,' *Language Arts* 59.

WEIR, R. (1962) *Language in the Crib*, The Hague, Mouton.

WELLS, C.G. (1974) 'Learning to code experience through language', *Journal Of Child Language*, 1.

WELLS, C.G. (1980) 'Adjustments in adult-child conversation: some effects of interaction', in GILES, H. *et al.* (Eds.) *Language: Social and Psychological Inspective*, Oxford, Pergamon.

WELLS, C.G. (1981) *Learning through interaction*, Cambridge, Cambridge University Press.

WELLS, C.G. (1984) *Language Development in the Pre-School Years*, Cambridge, Cambridge University Press.

WELLS, C.G. (in press) 'Pre-school literacy related activities and success in schools', in OLSON, D. (Ed.) *The Cognitive Consequences of Literacy*,

Cambridge, Cambridge University Press.

WELLS, C.G. NICHOLLS, J.C. (1980) 'The negotiation of meaning: talking and learning in the early years', *Working Papers in Language and Education*, 1, School of Education, University of East Anglia. (Subsequently published in *Analise Psicologica*, 1982, No. 1/2, series 3, pp. 85–102, Lisbon, Portugal).

WIDDOWSON, H. (1980) Open Lecture at Centre for Urban Educational Studies, Inner London Education Authority.

WILES, S. (1979) *The Multilingual Classroom*, in Open University Course PE 232, (Supplementary Readings, BLOCK 5) Milton Keynes, Open University Press.

WILES, S. (1981) 'Language Issues in the Multicultural Classroom', in MERCER, N. (1981) *Language in School and Community*, London, Arnold.

WILES, S. and FRANCE, P. (1983) *Working with Young Bilingual Children*, 4 programmes, Inner London Education Authority, Learning Resources Branch.

WILKINSON, A., BARNSLEY, G., HANNA, P. and SWAN, M. (1979). 'Assessing language development' *Language for Learning*, 1, 2, Language in Education Centre, University of Exeter, England, pp. 59–76.

WILKINSON, A., STRATTA, L. and DUDLEY, P. (1974) *The Quality of Listening*, London, Macmillan.

WILLIAMS, F. (Ed.) (1970) *Language and Poverty*, Chicago, Markham Publishing Company.

WOLL, B. (1978) 'Structure and function in language acquisition', in WATERSON, N. and SNOW, C. (Eds.) The Development of Communication, New York, Wiley, pp. 321–31.

WOOD, D. (1983) 'Teaching: natural and contrived', *Child Development Society Newsletter*, 31, pp. 2–7.

WOOD, D. in press, 'Talking to deaf children', *Proceedings of the 8th National Conference of the Australian Association for Special Education*, Department of Psychology, University of Nottingham, England.

WOODS, P. and HAMMERSLEY, M. (Eds.) (1977) *School Experience*, London, Croom Helm.

YOUNG, R. (Ed.) (1981) *Untying the Text*, London, Routledge and Kegan Paul.

Notes on Contributors

CARL BEREITER is a Professor at the Ontario Institute for Studies in Education, Toronto.

MARLENE SCARDAMALIA is an Associate Professor at York University, Toronto.

COURTNEY CAZDEN is a Professor in the Graduate School of Education at Harvard University.

PATRICIA CORDEIRO and MARY ELLEN GIACOBBE teach in New England schools and are members of the Harvard Graduate School of Education. Ms Giacobbe took part in the New Hampshire Writing Project.

TOM GORMAN is Head of the Department of Language at the National Foundation for Educational Research and Principal Research Officer of the APU language monitoring research team.

GUNTHER KRESS is Dean of the Faculty of Humanities and Social Studies, New South Wales Institute of Technology, Sydney, Australia.

MARGARET MEEK is a member of the Department of English Language at the University of London Institute of Education.

JOHN NICHOLLS, now retired, was formerly a member of the School of Education in the University of East Anglia, Norwich.

TERRY PHILLIPS is a Lecturer in the School of Education at the University of East Anglia.

GORDON WELLS is a Professor at the Ontario Institute for Studies in Education in Toronto and was previously Director of the Centre for the Study of Language and Communication at the University of Bristol.

SILVAINE WILES is Director of the Centre for Urban Educational Studies, Inner London Education Authority.

Index